EVERYDAY DISCIPLES

EVERYDAY DISCIPLES

COVENANT DISCIPLESHIP WITH YOUTH

CHRIS WILTERDINK

DISCIPLESHIP
RESOURCES

ISBNs
978-0-88177-793-2 (print)
978-0-88177-794-9 (mobi)
978-0-88177-795-6 (ePub)

EVERYDAY DISCIPLES: COVENANT DISCIPLESHIP WITH YOUTH

Library of Congress Control Number:

DR793

CONTENTS

INTRODUCTION

Everyday Things, Every Day

When we think about natural or human events that change the world, the easiest moments to recall are famous events or people that seemingly shock the world and things are different afterward. In history class, this would be called the great man theory. Popular in the 1800s (the same time that Methodism was booming in the United States), the theory said human history can largely be explained by the arrival of highly influential individuals that make change happen. The world is different because of Jesus or because of the apostle Paul. The world is different because of Genghis Khan. The world is different because of Mother Teresa, Martin Luther, Martin Luther King Jr., John Wesley, John Calvin, Rosa Parks . . . The world is also different because of the Indian Ocean tsunami in 2004, the Industrial Revolution, the 2011 earthquake in Japan, the Manhattan Project, the bubonic plague, famine, and many other natural or human-made events. The list could go on and on. Yet for their infamy, these people and events are just moments in the long timeline of God's relationship with people and the world.

Smaller acts, done regularly by many, actually shape our world and our lives in a much greater way than a handful of moments. Take, for example, the earthworm. These armless, legless creatures make a huge difference in shaping the world, through doing what they are designed to do every day. One earthworm can digest thirty-six tons of soil in one year, and in places where earthworms are common, an average of twenty-five worms live in a square foot of soil. That means about 2.5 million worms per hectare (about 2.5 acres) are just being worms: eating dirt and changing the shape of our world by moving more than forty-five metric tons of dirt a year! The world has about 1,386,000 hectares of farming land, so worms just doing their thing every day move over 6.2 billion metric tons of earth every year (Land Use table, A4, *FAO Statistical Yearbook*). Every year, worms move enough earth to equal the weight of 118 Great Pyramids of Giza!

World changers don't need to be big and famous; they need to live into their purpose every day. As people, we are created to be in relationship with God, to be stewards of the world and caretakers for our brothers and sisters. Covenant Discipleship is a way for people to do everyday things every day—and that leads to transformation. Yes, there will always be famous people or historical markers that define ages or generations, but the slow and steady process of salvation in the world happens because of everyday people doing everyday things every day.

Good News, Better News

There's an old joke that goes something like this: The good news is that there is a Messiah, a Savior. The better news is that it's not you!

The gospel of the life of Jesus is literally good news! So we take comfort in the fact that we are not the saviors of ourselves or the saviors of the world. God, through the life of Jesus and the presence of the Holy Spirit, has already provided that salvation. The better news is that we can be partners in grace. By living out Christ's teachings, we put ourselves more often into places where we can make a difference and differences are made in us. We are participants in God's kingdom.

The good news about covenants, discipleship, accountability, and the acts of compassion, justice, devotion, and worship is this: In some way, we are already doing them! We are keeping promises to others. We are living out some of Christ's teachings. We are accountable to others, and we are already trying to make the world a better place and better ourselves. Covenant Discipleship provides a framework and language for us to identify what we are already doing as disciples of Jesus Christ.

The better news then is that the support found in Covenant Discipleship groups improves the chances that the good things we do now become regular habits, and that those everyday habits have the potential to change the world and change who we are. This better news also means that Covenant Discipleship will keep us looking for new and different ways to live out our faith. Being in a Covenant Discipleship group keeps faith alive, healthy, growing, and dynamic. By sharing our own stories and experiences and listening to stories from others, the chances that we'll see God and experience Jesus in different ways are greatly improved.

An Introduction

Disciples who live by a covenant together are an "every day" people. They seek to honor God and love neighbor every day. Seemingly small everyday acts, when done every day, become the mustard seeds of faith that can move mountains. Everyday people doing everyday things every day can transform the world and themselves for the better.

Covenant Discipleship, as a concept and practice, adapts the accountability aspects of early Methodist class meetings. Today's Covenant Discipleship groups, for any age group, should not simply re-create a model of community from the 1800s. However, Covenant Discipleship groups for youth today should keep two important elements from John Wesley's original class meetings: mutual accountability and support. Young people thrive in connection, in communities of support. Covenants are sacred agreements between God and people that create relationships because of commitments to each other. Discipleship is an active following of Jesus' life and teachings. Patterning our own lives after the teachings of Jesus is no small feat. People are beings designed to be in community and relationship with each other. What better way, then, to pursue a life of discipleship than with the support and encouragement of a community?

Covenant Discipleship groups help encourage accountability and action for youth who seek to intentionally pattern their lives as Christians. Groups in which open discussion encourages members to better love God and love neighbor are a model way for young people to be active participants in their own discipleship journey. Covenants are God's way of being in community with humanity, and patterning our lives as disciples of Jesus Christ is one way to reply to God's call for relationship. John Wesley found that by combining covenants (offers of relationship initiated by God) with discipleship (a life patterned after Jesus' life and teachings) among small groups of Christians encouraged the participants in those groups to live more complete Christian lives—ones focused on personal and social transformation.

Members of a Covenant Discipleship group write a covenant with each other that outlines how each member of the group will live out his or her faith as a disciple. Then the group meets regularly to keep each other accountable to the promises participants have made, with the help of a class leader or guide. These groups help youth thrive in mutual accountability as they journey toward Christian perfection. They don't require space, don't require curriculum; they just require a little leadership to get going and a commitment from members to do everyday things every day. Regular meetings and consistent action create transformation over time, and the changes in a person and in a culture that come about because of intentionality can be incredible.

This resource is intended for adult leaders of youth who are committed to helping them grow as disciples of Jesus. Read on for a little insight into the history of Covenant Discipleship, an ideal way to live a more balanced Christian life. Use this resource in combination with the resources for adults and children, *Disciples Making Disciples: A Guide for Covenant Discipleship Groups and Class Leaders* by Steven W. Manskar, and *Growing Everyday Disciples: Covenant Discipleship with Children* by Melanie C. Gordon, Susan Groseclose, and Gayle Quay, to inspire your whole church to engage in this method of creating world-changing disciples of Jesus Christ. May John Wesley's words from "The Character of a Methodist" encourage you:

Is thy heart right, as my heart is with thine? I ask no farther question. If it be, give me thy hand. For opinions, or terms, let us not destroy the work of God. Dost thou love and serve God? It is enough. I give thee the right hand of fellowship. If there be any consolation in Christ, if any comfort of love, if any fellowship of the Spirit, if any bowels and mercies; let us strive together for the faith of the Gospel; walking worthy of the vocation wherewith we are called; with all lowliness and meekness, with long-suffering, forbearing one another in love, endeavouring to keep the unity of the Spirit in the bond of peace; remembering, there is one body, and one Spirit, even as we are called with one hope of our calling; "one Lord, one faith, one baptism; one God and Father of all, who is above all, and through all, and in you all."

CHAPTER 1

Learning from the Past—Seems Like Madness, But There's Method(ists) in It

Methodist history (like many parts of history) can be extremely boring, and Covenant Discipleship groups today should not seek to re-create something that worked in the 1700 and 1800s. However, knowing the roots of United Methodist faith expressions can provide some amazing insights. Today's Sunday school classes and small groups evolved from John Wesley's idea to bring groups of twelve or fewer people to "watch over one another in love" ("Advice to a People Called Methodist"). These groups formed communities within congregations that helped to keep Methodists mutually accountable to each other. This was incredibly important, as many early Methodist congregations had itinerant (mobile) pastors who traveled circuits and were not available on a weekly basis to directly care for their community. In today's world, The United Methodist Church has many communities without full-time pastors, much less full-time, paid staff responsible solely for ministry with youth. Covenant Discipleship is a way for youth to grow spiritually while growing in community, under the guidance of their peers and other leaders in the congregation.

John Wesley was a minister in the Church of England. He saw a church that was missing the opportunity to be in ministry with people who were poor and disconnected from their surrounding communities. His message that people could become participants in their own salvation by doing works of piety and mercy was well received. (*Piety* means things that a person does to support his or her personal holiness. *Mercy* means things that a person does to support social holiness, or social good.) The system of weekly meetings where Methodists would discover "how their souls prospered" created a sustainable group that wasn't tied to the best preacher, the latest worship music, or having the best-kept facilities. They were groups that could thrive among rich and poor, in buildings or in fields, because of the commitments people kept to each other (Iovino, "How's Your Spiritual Life? The Class Meeting for Today").

> The most profitable exercise of any is a free inquiry into the state of the heart.
> —FRANCIS ASBURY

Methodism grew like crazy in the United States between 1776 and 1850. In 1850 over 34 percent of religious adherents were Methodist and each of them was expected to participate in a weekly class meeting (Fink and Stark, *The Churching of America, 1776–2005*, page 16)! This connection provided immediate accountability and support for those new to faith. New Methodists could both grow in their faith and practice (in every sense of that word) their faith alongside more established members of congregations.

Today youth have an increasingly diverse set of social circles begging for their participation, and the world invites them into a life of complexity. Social circles such as friend groups at school, peers in extracurricular activities and teams, and friends and mentors at church are among the circles familiar to other generations. Newer social circles include the networks that form among those using technology. These social circles are often larger, more diverse, and more complex to navigate than the in-person circles. They also expose youth to wider sets of beliefs and opinions as young people form their identities and grow into adulthood. Social circles are important for development and, of course, will always have a place in the lives of young people. However, Covenant Discipleship groups are more than just another social circle.

Covenant Discipleship groups meet together expecting transformation, both of the self and of the world. They are not Bible studies, not places of judgment, not a group that gets together to complete the latest and greatest curriculum. (In fact, Covenant

Discipleship groups can help ministries break away from addictions to curriculum, saving money by investing in the possibility of more transformation rather than more information!) They are groups that help youth interpret the culture around them and bring their faith into their whole lives, providing them with support to live as Christians. Ultimately, Covenant Discipleship groups are safe places youth can voice their experience of God. They are groups where the goal isn't to know the most stuff about God, Jesus, or the Bible. Instead the goal in Covenant Discipleship groups is to share deeply about living in Christ and the actions taken to gain the mind that was in Christ Jesus.

> Beware you be not swallowed up in books! An ounce of love is worth a pound of knowledge.
> —JOHN WESLEY, LETTERS OF JOHN WESLEY

That said, it can feel uncomfortable for youth (or anyone, really) to be in a group where the expectations include sharing about their personal relationship with God. The average social circle doesn't demand any more of its participants than showing up and doing the same thing together (Hey, let's go bowling!). A Covenant Discipleship group asks for presence, yes. It also asks for everyone to do the same thing (live an active faith). In addition, the group asks for participants to be accountable to each other and to create a covenant of behaviors each member will try to accomplish every week. Mutual accountability in a Covenant Discipleship group shouldn't imply that members judge the behaviors of others in the group, but instead they focus their time together on stories of how members of the group have lived their faith in the past week. As Kevin Watson notes in *The Class Meeting*, "The primary person judging you in a [mutually accountable group] should be yourself" (page 139). Having group members share answers to questions such as "How has my week gone?"

> We should be rigorous in judging ourselves and gracious in judging others.
> —JOHN WESLEY

or "What have I done or not done to live into our group's covenant?" demonstrates a willingness to be present and share, not to judge. Being part of a Covenant Discipleship group is not about having the right information or answers based on reading curriculum. It is about people intentionally creating chances to represent Jesus in the world. It is about sharing how those experiences continually shape and form us as disciples.

Discipleship

The earliest of Jesus' followers began to discover life in Christ because of a two-word invitation—"Follow me" (Matt. 4:18-22; John 1:35-43). Simply put, discipleship is a way of living that follows the life and teachings of Jesus Christ. The original disciples often called Jesus "Rabbi," which means teacher. In their time and place, learning from a rabbi and following a rabbi were literally the same thing. The disciples learned by following their rabbi, Jesus, from town to town. They would eat, sleep, pray, laugh, walk, argue, and learn over the course of three years together. *For disciples, learning means going where the teacher goes.* By going where Jesus went, the disciples learned as Jesus taught and lived as Jesus lived, totally immersed in the presence of their teacher. In this way, they learned the greatest commandments, "Love your enemies and pray for those who persecute you" (Matt. 5:44), "You shall love the Lord your God with all your heart, and with all your soul, and with all your mind. . . . You shall love your neighbor as yourself" (Matt. 22:37, 39), and "Love one another. Just as I have loved you, you also should love one another" (John 13:34).

Today, being a disciple still means following where the teacher leads. So where is Jesus most likely to be found today? In the same kind of company Pharisees complained about him spending time with back in the day (Luke 15:2; Mark 2:15-16). Jesus identified himself among the outcasts: "Truly I tell you, just as you did it to one of the least of these who are members of my family, you did it to me" (Matt. 25:40). Today's disciples need to find those who are vulnerable, voiceless, poor, and despised and immerse themselves in service. John Wesley also saw the need to get outside church walls and meet the needs of poor people in the community (more on that in the "Methodist Briefs" section below). Actions like these are called works of mercy and will help covenant disciples demonstrate their love for neighbor.

Philippians 2:5 calls disciples to "let the same mind be in you that was in Christ Jesus," so living a life of discipleship also means becoming familiar with Jesus' life and teachings. That familiarity can be gained by reading and studying the Bible. Yes, disciples read scripture. Yes, disciples use tools and resources outside the Bible to help understand what is inside the Bible. Disciples also pray, take Communion, and seek to live a healthy and balanced life. Covenant disciples can call these things works of piety. Actions like these help demonstrate love for God. Many works of piety and mercy can be accomplished as an individual, while some are best done in community.

Discipleship means being part of a community, acting as a part of the body of Christ (1 Cor. 12:12-14). Disciples are Christ's ambassadors in the world (2 Cor. 5:20) and can recognize themselves as members of God's family (Eph. 1:3-14; 2:19-22; Rom. 8:14-17; Gal. 4:4-7). A life of discipleship is a life that reflects Jesus as a teacher and brother. The communal aspect of a disciple's journey links the earliest followers of Christ with the youth of today in the social religion that is Christianity.

Covenants

The concept of covenant can be confusing because of the temptation to simplify the term into more familiar elements. Some view covenants as contracts, where two (or more) parties voluntarily make an agreement to provide something as long as certain conditions are met. Think about how a data company will promise to connect devices (mobile phones, tablets, and so forth) to their network and provide the ability to make phone calls, send text messages, and access data as long as a person pays the amount owed for that connection. If either the company or the person breaks the contract, there will be legal consequences or financial fines. Contracts are often tied to things.

Some view covenants as promises, commitments to do or not do something. Promises can be made with oneself, with another person, even between groups of people. Promises can be broken and are always tied to an action. The consequences of breaking a promise aren't always legal, but they can have a major effect on trust. Picture a friend not showing up when he said he would, a politician who promised changes in government but kept things status quo when she got into office, a sibling who promised to keep a secret but ended up spilling the beans. People are not things, and the relationships we keep up in community rely on trust. Covenants often contain promises, but they go a step beyond the promises we normally make.

With discipleship, a covenant is about more than things or actions that people can promise to give. *A covenant is a relationship initiated by God that people can respond to by living a life of discipleship.* God's covenant of unconditional love and grace with humanity provides people the opportunity to be active participants, overcoming sin and death in the process. God is in relationship with people through covenant, and while the making and keeping of promises is an important element of that relationship, God's covenant is larger than a contract or promise. God's covenant is one where grace goes before us, surrounds us in life, and works in us and through our communities. We are born into God's covenant of grace, and when we recognize that gift, we have the chance to respond to it by living a life of discipleship.

The Bible shows us that God covenants with individuals, with groups of people, and with all of creation. With every covenant, God establishes a relationship to meet the human needs of community. People desire to find order in the midst of seeming chaos, to explore creation and name new things, to express curiosity at the world around us. People often desire to do those things with others, not alone—and those needs are expressed in the covenant with Adam and Eve in Eden (Gen. 1:28-30; 2:15-17). We know this first story of covenant came to a difficult end for people with the whole "fruit of the tree of knowledge of good and evil" escapade (Gen. 3:14-19), but even that part of the covenant serves the notion of community. Even as God exiled Adam and Eve from the garden, God sent them out together. Even in moments where people fall short, God offers them community and the opportunity for a new and different life. People are not perfect and are allowed to make mistakes, to fall short of expectations. Actually, we could read the whole Bible as the story of God establishing relationship with people and calling on them to live as image bearers of the God who created them, followed by people repeatedly messing up, then people finding redemption through community with each other and in relationship with God.

God calls us on toward perfection and to work hard to set things right, not to hide from mistakes we make (like Adam and Eve, who jumped behind the bushes when God showed up in the garden). God's commitment to have humanity continue to become the best version of itself through community continues in the covenants with Noah (Gen. 9:1-17), Abraham and Sarah (Gen. 12:1-3), and Moses (Exod. 20:1-17). God is with Noah's family as they bring abundance back to the earth. God blesses all families and communities through Abraham, even in the midst of his own family's struggles. In sharing the commandments with Moses and the Israelites at Mount Sinai, God lays out a new set of rules for people to be in community with each other and with God.

God has a need for relationship and community, just like people do—after all, we are image bearers of God! In every covenant, God is faithful to God's Word. In covenants of relationship and community, God associates with the oppressed (Moses), sees misery (Adam and Eve), and hears cries of his children (Abraham and Sarah). In prophecies about the new covenant the Messiah will establish (Jer. 31:31-34), God will move from seeing and hearing human needs to knowing human needs. God becomes flesh in Jesus, knowing what it is to be human by being human. The person of Jesus makes

God vulnerable and willing to share in human suffering. This reaffirms the relationship God wants to create with people through covenant. A God "wounded for our transgressions, . . . and by his bruises we are healed" establishes a new covenant in the life of Jesus by knowing pain, joy, temptation, thirst, satisfaction, and death (Isa. 53:5).

When asked about the law, and therefore the earlier covenants that God had made with people, Jesus recasts the earlier covenants using the language of love: "Jesus answered, 'The first is, "Hear, O Israel: the Lord our God, the Lord is one; you shall love the Lord your God with all your heart, and with all your soul, and with all your mind, and with all your strength." The second is this, "You shall love your neighbor as yourself." There is no other commandment greater than these'" (Mark 12:29-31). The life of Christ is the new covenant, and his invitation is to "follow me." When we choose to live a life of discipleship, patterning our behavior after Jesus' life and teachings, we accept God's new covenant and Jesus' call to follow him. In a life of discipleship, we live into the new covenant by doing all we do in remembrance of Jesus and enjoy a permanent and unbroken relationship with God (Heb. 9:15).

Methodist Briefs

Methodism began as a movement to inspire and train disciples for Christian living and to spread scriptural holiness. John Wesley started the Methodist movement (1738) about two hundred years after Martin Luther began the Protestant Reformation (1517). John saw his own church, the Church of England, as limiting who it served to the educated, the wealthy, and the cultured people of the day, not the commoners. This bothered John enough that he began preaching out in fields and other places where the working class could be found. During his time at the University of Oxford, he also participated in regular meetings of a group called the Holy Club. He and other students would meet to read, study scripture, and examine their lives as Christians.

In this way, Wesley's concept of Covenant Discipleship is rooted in young people. The Holy Club at Oxford may very well be the first Covenant Discipleship group in the Methodist movement, and it was made up of young people! Disciples helping each other ensure that every hour of their day had purpose became foundational in Wesley's call for Christians to couple action with their beliefs as Methodists.

These groups originally had several different structures and names including classes, bands, and societies. Wesley claimed that forming classes arose out of the need to organize large numbers of people who had flocked to this new movement, and these smaller groups also facilitated other practical expressions of faith, such as collecting money to pay off debts or to support the needs of poor people.

Class, Band, and Society Meetings

Classes, bands, and societies took different shapes and priorities in Britain and in the Americas. Yet, even though they developed in different ways, they remained an integral part of the early Methodist movement in both places. Francis Asbury, who literally saw all of the Methodist Episcopal Church in America as he rode horses over enormous circuits in the late 1700s and early 1800s, noted that he rarely met a deeply committed Christian who was not involved in something like the class meeting. These early Methodists, after all, were asked not only to make a commitment to grow in grace themselves but also to invite others into their life and grow in community.

> Never omit meeting your Class or Band. . . . These are the very sinews of our Society; and whatever weakens, or tends to weaken, our regard for these, or our exactness in attending them, strikes at the very root of our community.
>
> —JOHN WESLEY

Asbury's time as a superintendent of the Methodists in America coincided with an explosion of growth in the Methodist church. One major factor in that growth was the use of classes, bands, and societies. Methodism in the United States grew from 2.5 percent of religious adherents in 1776 all the way to 34.2 percent in 1850; one-third of the United States was Methodist in 1850 (Watson, *The Class Meeting*)! Societies, bands, and classes were ways of organizing and creating accountability in a time where Methodist preachers traveled circuits and local congregations of Methodists did not see their pastor every week.

In the United States, a *society* became synonymous with a *congregation*—a group that meets together to worship on Sundays. Societies came in all shapes and sizes, just like church congregations today.

Bands were small groups of up to seven people. These groups were voluntary, and specifically for people who already had deep spiritual commitments to Christ and could identify an experience of "new birth." Bands grouped people by gender, age range, and spiritual maturity. They focused intensely on confession as a means of becoming more holy.

Classes organized into groups of up to twelve people. Participation in a class, as a part of identifying as a Methodist, was required by both John Wesley and Francis Asbury. A class met once a week and brought together new Methodists and established members to "watch over one another in love" with the guidance of a class leader.

The Covenant Discipleship groups for youth outlined and explored in this resource have pieces in common with historical band and class meetings, but they are not exact replicas of these older types of gatherings.

TL; DR (Too Long; Didn't Read) Page

- Ministry in communities of twelve or fewer people has been common in Methodism ever since the beginning of the movement. They had slightly different sizes and makeups, but were consistently organized into groups called classes, bands, or societies.

- The founders of Methodism saw participation in these groups as integral to a person's faith, because they made a space for people to ask each other how they were putting their faith into action and ask, how is it with your soul?

- Social networks and clubs that prioritize and emphasize a place of belonging have always been important in the lives of young people.

- Covenant Discipleship groups provide a structure to reflect upon intentional Christian actions.

- Discipleship is a way of following the teachings of Christ and patterning a life after the life that Jesus lived. Mark 12:29-31 sums up what a life of discipleship looks like: to love God and to love neighbor.

- Covenants are God's way of being in relationship with humanity; they are sacred promises. In a life of discipleship, we live into a new covenant with God by doing all we do in remembrance of Jesus and enjoy a permanent and unbroken relationship with God (Heb. 9:15).

- Covenant Discipleship combines God's way of relating to people with the opportunity to pattern a life after Christ.

- Groups of disciples who covenant to pattern their actions to intentionally act out Christ's teachings create opportunities to develop deeper relationships with each other, with God, and with their communities.

- The good news: Methodism has a proud history of world-changing disciples meeting in small groups to support each other. Those small groups and their structure were originally dreamed up and attended by young people.

- The better news: The social nature of these small groups keeps them relevant for young people today, and they create a safe space for young Christians to "practice what they preach."

CHAPTER 2

Covenant Discipleship: Common Methods, Uncommon Results

Joining the concepts of covenant (God's way of being in relationship with humanity) and discipleship (living out the teachings and life of Jesus) together into Covenant Discipleship creates the opportunity for youth to be in relationship with each other, and with God, as they live out a Christ-centered life. The beginning of a life of discipleship, for John Wesley, was marked by a covenant—the baptismal covenant: "Through the Sacrament of Baptism we are initiated into Christ's holy church. We are incorporated into God's mighty acts of salvation and given new birth through water and the Spirit. All this is God's gift, offered to us without price" ("Baptismal Covenant I," *The United Methodist Hymnal*, page 33).

John Wesley called baptism "an outward sign of God's gift of inward grace." Baptism is an act of God through the grace of Jesus Christ and the work of the Holy Spirit. In The United Methodist Church, infants are baptized because the congregation is called to help nurture and form that child's faith life, though a person can be baptized anytime. Methodists believe that one baptism is enough—essentially God gets it right the first time! We can celebrate and remember our baptisms always, but the UMC does not believe a "rebaptism" is necessary to live a life of discipleship, since God's grace is constantly surrounding us. As a person is baptized, the community participates in a covenant to love and care for a new sister or brother in Christ and walk in the way that leads to life.

One reason the Methodist movement became so popular in the United States was the common method that all covenant groups used to explore and express their faith. A group of twelve people, or fewer, would share how they were following Jesus' teachings and support each other in their Christian journey. This method led to the uncommon growth of Methodism and the transformation of both individuals and communities.

The General Rule of Discipleship

The intentional actions that follow a baptismal covenant are built around what Methodists call the General Rule of Discipleship, which is "to witness to Jesus Christ in the world and to follow His teachings through acts of compassion, justice, worship, and devotion under the guidance of the Holy Spirit" (*The Book of Discipline of The United Methodist Church 2008*, ¶ 1118.2).

John Wesley's sermon "On God's Vineyard," among other things, looked at the common practices of Methodists in England and Wales. Wesley was proud of how his Methodists were thriving in mutual accountability through class meetings, and he shared the secret of how a diverse body of believers was able to make such strides in their own discipleship by following three simple rules for living. These rules have been explored fully in many writings, with *Three Simple Rules That Will Change the World* by Rueben Job being a well-known example.

John Wesley's General Rules are as follows:

First: By doing no harm, by avoiding evil of every kind, especially that which is most generally practiced. . . .

Secondly: By doing good; by being in every kind merciful after their power; as they have opportunity, doing good of every possible sort, and, as far as possible, to all men:

To their bodies, of the ability which God gives, by giving food to the hungry, by clothing the naked, by visiting or helping them that are sick or in prison. To their souls, by instructing, reproving, or exhorting all we have any intercourse with; trampling under foot that enthusiastic doctrine that "we are not to do good unless our hearts be free to it.". . . By running with patience the race which is set before them, denying themselves, and taking up their cross daily; submitting to bear the reproach of Christ, to be as the filth and offscouring of the world; and looking that men should say all manner of evil of them falsely, for the Lord's sake.

Thirdly:
By attending upon all the ordinances of God; such are:

- The public worship of God.
- The ministry of the Word, either read or expounded.
- The Supper of the Lord.
- Family and private prayer.
- Searching the Scriptures.
- Fasting or abstinence.

These are the General Rules of our societies; all of which we are taught of God to observe, even in his written Word, which is the only rule, and the sufficient rule, both of our faith and practice. And all these we know his Spirit writes on truly awakened hearts. (*The Book of Discipline of The United Methodist Church 2008*, ¶ 103, emphasis added)

Those rules are meant to guide the purposeful actions we take as Christians trying to answer Christ's call to take up the cross and follow him (Luke 9:23). They are not laws, but they are guides, intentionally left open to allow for innovation, creativity, and discovery of Christ under the guidance of the Holy Spirit. Wesley's rules for discipleship are specific and call for action, but how we carry out the actions of witnessing for Jesus Christ in the world is not narrow or limited. This mirrors the open-ended calls to action in Jesus' Great Commandment to love the Lord your God with all our heart, soul, mind and to love our neighbor as ourselves (Matt. 22:37, 39).

Balanced Discipleship

John 3:16 is among the most famous scriptures and speaks to the giving nature of God. God's love for the world became a person in Jesus Christ. Disciples share that good news by living as Christ lived. The words and actions we choose to share with our communities, because of our faith, are often the first way people begin to understand what Jesus is all about. If John Wesley were alive today, he may well encourage us to be "everyday people." By that I mean that a Wesleyan faith encourages us to grow and be the living body of Christ by doing everyday things every day. Being a disciple isn't a static life where nothing ever changes, but a life where we can grow in grace in community and where our faith is integrated into our daily lives—not limited to two hours on a Sunday in a sanctuary or church building.

The everyday things we can do sound extraordinary in scripture! Bringing good news to the poor, releasing captives, opening the eyes of the blind, and liberating the oppressed (Luke 4:16-18); feeding the hungry, quenching the thirsty, clothing the naked, welcoming the homeless stranger, visiting the sick and prisoners (Matt. 25:37-40); loving one another as Christ loves us (John 13:34-35); loving God and loving neighbor as self (Matt. 22:34-40). These things are extraordinary expressions of care, which we have the opportunity to do every day. God provides opportunities every day for us to become a dynamic, moving expression of God's love for the world. The spirit of the living God becomes even more obvious when we do those everyday things together, in community.

Covenant Discipleship groups invite Methodists into each other's lives to grow in grace with each other's support, thriving in mutual accountability. Having a friend and fellow Christian regularly ask, "How is your life with God?" challenges a person to be active in living out his or her faith. That question also becomes a lot easier to answer when people can point to specific actions that they've been intentional about doing! John Wesley preached that we could live into the General Rule of Discipleship by following the Great Commandment of Matthew 22:37, 39—love God and love neighbor. We express our love for God by works of piety and we express our love for neighbor through works of mercy.

An image that can help organize the actions of a disciple trying to intentionally do works of piety and mercy is the Jerusalem cross. As you read this section, picture yourself at the center of this cross, always centered on the life of Jesus. The arms of the cross represent where you'll reach out into the world and deeper into yourself, yet always remain connected to that center. These actions create a balanced approach to living as a disciple.

Works of Mercy, Works of Piety

Loving Neighbor: Works of Mercy

A work of mercy is something that we choose to do that shows the love of God to our neighbor, transforming the world through grace. Works of mercy extend God's love to serve the spiritual, physical, and material needs of others and can be done by a single person (personal) or together with others (public). Both in scriptures and in Wesleyan tradition, these acts include caring for widows, orphans, strangers, and those who are naked, hungry, and imprisoned (Zech. 7:10; Matt. 25:31-46). Showing love and care for our neighbors works toward what John Wesley would call social holiness. In Wesley's definition, works of mercy are further categorized as acts of compassion and acts of justice. *Acts of compassion* are actions that meet the needs of the neighbor, anyone that that we encounter who is in need. Matthew 25:35-36 shares Jesus' reminder that whatever we do to the least of these, we do to Jesus. As disciples, we need to be out in the world, putting ourselves in the presence of Christ himself. We not only serve people who are poor but also are in community with them; we get to know them, learn their names and their stories. Only then will we truly be able to understand their needs. John 13:34-35 states that everyone will know his disciples by the love they show. We show that love of Christ by our intentional presence in the places where Christ is most likely to be found, among the poorest and least in our communities.

See chapter 3 for suggestions about *acts of compassion* (doing good works, visiting those who are sick, visiting those in prison, feeding the hungry, and more) to consider in your congregation and community.

Acts of justice are actions that address the causes of a neighbor's suffering. These acts of discipleship include asking questions about systems and climates that contribute to poverty. An act of compassion would be buying lunch for a hungry family. An act of justice would be investigating why that family was hungry and addressing the institutional or cultural issues causing that family to struggle with hunger. Deuteronomy 10:18; Psalm 10:18; Isaiah 58:1-12; 61:1-2; and Jeremiah 5:28 help us understand that justice means acting on behalf of all so that everyone in a society can live and fully participate in their society.

See chapter 3 for suggestions about *acts of justice* (ending oppression and discrimination, addressing the needs of people who are poor, and more) to consider in your congregation and community.

Loving God: Works of Piety

A work of piety is something that we choose to do to that invites God's grace to transform us personally. Works of piety are things people can do by themselves (personal) or together (public) to express their love for God and (to use John Wesley's terms) work toward personal holiness. Check out Luke 11:37-43. Jesus uses the image of a dirty cup as a metaphor for one's outward appearance versus inward reality. The metaphor is about having our actions, what we say and do to others, match our inner beliefs. Works of piety open our hearts to grace and help keep us connected to Christ. Works of piety help grace flow through us, reminding and encouraging us to act like Christ in the world. In Wesley's definition, works of piety are further categorized as acts of worship and acts of devotion.

Acts of worship are actions that publicly reveal ourselves to God. They are things we must do in community with others. Acts of worship are what most people think of when they think of church: worship, singing hymns, praying together, hearing sermons, taking Communion—public ways to embrace our devotion to God. The actions in worship bind us together in love with all the disciples who came before us, in part because we repeat meaningful rituals together. The worship we're talking about here is worship where disciples are present together, celebrating common bonds, honestly engaged together to experience forgiveness and fellowship. It's not the kind public prayer showing off that Jesus warns about in Matthew 6:1, 5—it is genuine time spent in community giving thanks for all that God has done and is doing.

See chapter 3 for suggestions about specific *acts of worship* (public worship and Communion, receiving and exploring God's Word together, and sharing faith) to consider in your congregation and community.

Acts of devotion are actions that keep up our personal relationship with God. They are the things we do individually. Different prayer practices, meditation, journaling, fasting, and studying scripture can help us center our lives on Christ and our relationship with God through covenant. Just like a productive garden, our personal relationship with Christ needs regular care. Picture yourself as the gardener in Luke 8:4-8, spreading seeds that fall upon different kinds of ground. Not every act of devotion we do is going to take root, bloom, and transform the garden that is our relationship with Christ—but we shouldn't be selective with the seeds we plant, nor where we plant them. When we are generous with the time we devote to our relationship with Christ, we'll start to see transformations in unexpected places.

See chapter 3 for suggestions about specific *acts of devotion* (spending time with scripture, praying, and fasting) to consider in your personal life.

Covenants and Accountability

Participating in the mutual accountability of a Covenant Discipleship group can be a paradigm-shifting experience in which, once the experience begins, youth see the rest of life differently.

It is important for the young people in a Covenant Discipleship to join because they want to; that they say yes to the opportunity to be present, consent to the covenant that will be followed, and affirm their status as equals within the group. The word *mutual* means a partnership, a shared experience in which everyone voluntarily participates.

We are used to being accountable to someone with authority. Students are accountable to a teacher, children are accountable to parents, players are accountable to a coach, and so on. Yet, in Covenant Discipleship, participants are accountable to each other. A sense of freedom and responsibility emerges when authority in the group is leveled. Disciples in covenant together become mutually accountable to each other. A close example from school life in the United States is the marching band. They have a conductor (like the youth minister) who oversees the entirety of the band from a distance. The band is divided into sections with section leaders (like class leaders or guides) by instrument, and then those sections each do different things to make music and sometimes create elaborate designs as they march. Individuals in a marching band know their place and what direction to march based upon the people next to them, their neighbors. When a member of a marching band misses practice or a performance, the show still goes on— but the music is missing a few notes and some volume, and the creative design of any shape becomes incomplete. Their absence is noticeable, by others in the marching band and also to the community watching the performance. Marching band members rely on their neighbors to help them know where to be and what to do, and by doing so create tremendous, moving pieces of art.

Covenant disciples also rely on each other to discern where to be and what to do, to live into Christ's teachings, and to transform each other and transform the world. Becoming mutually accountable involves a commitment to be present in a Covenant Discipleship group, to help create and then live out a covenant created by the group. This process creates a circular and repeating pattern where we live Christ's teachings, learn in relationship with others, experience God through our actions, then witness to the differences we've seen because of those experiences.

> Live Christ's teachings
> Learn in relationship with others
> Experience God through our actions
> Witness to the differences seen because of those experiences

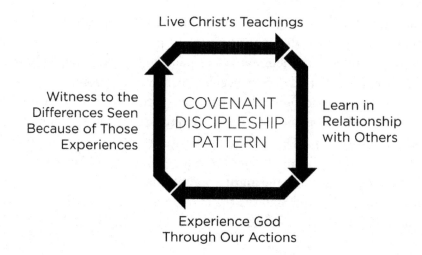

Live Christ's Teachings

Witness to the Differences Seen Because of Those Experiences

COVENANT DISCIPLESHIP PATTERN

Learn in Relationship with Others

Experience God Through Our Actions

Being in a Covenant Discipleship group is more than a résumé builder. It's about being an agent of transformation who is transformed by living out faith. It combats isolation, builds relationships, and creates regular times and ways of connecting with peers and with those who are poor. Covenant discipleship is a system that provides accountability and support as we seek to become better Christians while looking for Jesus on the margins of society.

Forming a Covenant

Each Covenant Discipleship group creates its own covenant, a collective promise of what each member of the group will do on a weekly basis to be better disciples of Jesus Christ. A basic covenant is made up of three parts: the preamble, the clauses, and the conclusion.

- Preamble: states why the covenant exists and the commitment for the group
- Clauses: state specific goals for individuals and the group
- Conclusion: a pledge of commitment and reminder of grace

The United Methodist Church is built upon covenants. Our lives as disciples, constantly bettering ourselves by living like Christ, are a response to baptism. The Methodist church tradition is to baptize infants. Baptism is a sacrament that signifies God originating the process of salvation, both for the infant and for the community taking part in the baptism. The baptismal vows of the UMC start with this sentence: "Through the Sacrament of Baptism, we are initiated into Christ's holy Church." Baptism is the trampoline that launches all the other works of piety and mercy into the world. Yes, we could do any or all of the means of grace without being baptized. They would still make a difference in the world, a difference to us, and a difference in the lives of others. But when we look at baptism as a starting point, everything else we do for our faith is a response to that baptism. Baptism marks the beginning of a journey we walk in community with others, toward being a more perfect version of ourselves by living in Christ. When we practice the means of grace in a community that has entered into a baptismal covenant with us, we go on to transform the world surrounded by that same community that will encircle us with prayer, love, and forgiveness. It's a community of promises that equip us to become the persons God created us to be! We state in the *Services of the Baptismal Covenant* (pages 5, 10):

With God's help we will proclaim the good news and live according to the example of Christ. We will surround these persons with a community of love and forgiveness, that they may grow in their trust of God, and be found faithful in their service to others. We will pray for them, that they may be true disciples who walk in the way that leads to life. . . .

We give thanks for all that God has already given you and we welcome you in Christian love. As members together with you in the body of Christ and in this congregation of The United Methodist Church, we renew our covenant faithfully to participate in the ministries of the Church by our prayers, our presence, our gifts, our service and our witness, that in everything God may be glorified through Jesus Christ.

In that baptismal covenant, a community promises to support the family and the infant as they grow in faith. From the beginning of our relationship with the church, we are called to be mutually accountable and supportive of others. Covenant Discipleship is a formal way of becoming mutually accountable to a small group and living out those baptismal vows in new ways.

Being Accountable

Observations by the American Psychological Association (http://www.apa.org/helpcenter /lifestyle-changes.aspx) show that when people want to create lasting changes in their lives or behavior the support of other people and keeping accountability are two of the most important factors. Most people look at accountability in one of three ways: personal, authoritative, or mutual. To explore each one, let's take the example of a person preparing for a 5K race.

- *Personal accountability*: A person makes a decision, doesn't share that decision with anyone else, and motivates or tracks only her own accomplishments. Our runner decides to take part in a 5K race, but she doesn't tell anybody else about her plans. She makes a plan to start training and to get in shape, maybe buys the appropriate gear, and starts preparing. Some people can stay self-motivated enough to accomplish their goal and get fit enough to complete the 5K. For others, once the excitement of doing something new fades, it can be difficult to stay motivated. If the goal of participating in the race is in danger of not being met, the only person to know or encourage a different result is the runner herself.

- *Authoritative accountability*: A person makes a decision (or a decision gets made for him or her!), and another individual, such as a coach, parent, or teacher (or even God!), makes sure that the person lives into the decision. Our runner will still do the 5K race, but now a coach will come up with a training plan and will regularly check on the runner to make sure that she is keeping up with her training and preparation. The coach knows the goal just as much as the runner does and can help motivate the runner and keep her on track. However, the coach isn't trying to run the 5K race; the coach's goal in the relationship is to motivate and inspire, but not to run the race alongside our runner.
- *Mutual accountability*: Several people and runners make a decision together and pledge to support each other in preparation and action. Now our runner talks with others about her goal of running the 5K race, and they also happen to be interested in running it. They plan training runs with each other, share how they are feeling, and get ready for the race together. Every person motivates each other, grows together, sees the same challenges, works toward the same goal.

Covenant Discipleship is a commitment to mutual accountability, to run the race of Hebrews 12:1-3 together, helping others keep their eyes fixed on Jesus—the pioneer and perfecter of our faith. Running involves training, and having a group that will motivate us to get out of bed and train, even on the days when muscles are sore or our eyes are tired, is an invaluable gift that will improve how well each one runs the race. Likewise, we'll cheer on other members of the group as we run toward the same goal—collaborative and cooperative, not competitive.

Covenant Discipleship is not competitive Christianity, a place where people brag to each other about their faith, their devotion, or their actions. It is a place for cooperation and support, where all members of the group seek to better themselves and their faith by specifically doing acts of compassion, justice, devotion, and worship. It's a strategy to race well and to care for others in the process.

TL; DR Page

- Every action we choose to do as Christians is a response to our baptism and the baptismal covenant congregations promise on our behalf.
- The General Rule of Discipleship is "to witness to Jesus Christ in the world and to follow His teachings through acts of compassion, justice, worship, and devotion under the guidance of the Holy Spirit" (*The Book of Discipline of The United Methodist Church 2008*, ¶ 1118.2).
- Rules for living:
  - Do no harm.
  - Do good.
  - Tend to the ordinances of God.
- Being a disciple means using these rules to guide the development of an active and dynamic faith. The rules are a way to organize our faithful responses to Jesus' call to "love God and love neighbor" into four categories: acts of compassion, justice, worship, and devotion.
- Acts of justice and compassion are both works of mercy. They are things we can do to show our love of neighbor.
- Acts of worship and devotion are both works of piety. They are the things we can do to show our love of God.

- Compassion and devotion are the acts that people can do personally, as individuals. Justice and worship are the acts that people can do in groups and in community.
- The Jerusalem cross provides a helpful way to picture a balanced life of discipleship.
- Intentionally doing personal and public works of mercy and piety makes a life of balanced discipleship that helps a disciple stay centered on the cross.
- Covenant Discipleship provides the opportunity to experience mutual accountability and to be an active participant in spiritual growth.
- Covenants are customizable, and each group creates their own covenant that includes a preamble, four to ten clauses, and a conclusion.
- Covenant discipleship can be looked at as a way to run the race referred to in Hebrews 12:1-3. Participants in a group are each other's training partners, supporting their brothers and sisters in Christ while running the race alongside them. The race isn't competitive but collaborative.
- The world can be changed by everyday people doing everyday things every day. In essence, the Methodist movement calls us to shape the world and ourselves through regular activities that intentionally connect us with God, by doing the work of Jesus, with the support of the Holy Spirit.

CHAPTER 3

Planning Your Doing: Ideas for Developing Discipleship Habits

Covenant Discipleship groups help people continue to do what they are already doing, learn about new ways of being a faithful disciple through works of mercy and piety, and commit to do both old and new things regularly. Doing everyday things every day can have profound impacts on our faith and on the world.

By recognizing what we already do as faithful disciples, we can celebrate with each other as we put our faith into action. Many of us are already doing something, and for those opportunities and energy, we are grateful.

By recognizing that we don't (and actually can't!) do all the works of piety and mercy all the time, we can support new growth by identifying things we want to learn more about. Being with others who can also admit that they don't know everything or can't do everything creates an open environment where covenant disciples thrive in mutual accountability.

By committing to doing something we already do more regularly, or committing to taking on something new, we intentionally develop our faith lives and improve the world. Research shows that if a person can commit to doing something regularly for six weeks and following through with that commitment, then it becomes a habit. Creating new habits eventually makes more space to take on new and different actions!

Doing Works of Mercy

Works of mercy include acts of compassion and justice. Acts of compassion are private and include doing good works, visiting those who are sick, visiting those in prison, and feeding the hungry. Acts of justice are public and include ending oppression and discrimination and addressing the needs of people who are poor.

Acts of COMPASSION

Acts of compassion are personal or private actions that reflect Jesus' command to love our neighbor as ourselves.

Doing Good Works

God's grace sustains us while we do good works, but what exactly are good works? They are things done to show love to a neighbor (external action) because of our love for God (internal motivation). We are motivated by our love of God to do good works for our neighbors. Good works are "good" for several reasons. First, they do good for our spiritual lives. John Wesley connected grace, faith, and works as a way we can live a full Christian life. Second, when we do good, both we and the world are transformed through God's grace. An element of the doing shapes our faith and inspires us to further action, because we are exposed to more needs in this hurting world. When we do good, it means we have taken the time and energy to discover the needs of another, we've thought about something larger than ourselves, and we've invested ourselves in making a difference.

> Our gospel, as it knows no other foundation of good works than faith, or of faith than Christ, so it clearly informs us, we are not his disciples while we either deny him to be the Author, or his Spirit to be the Inspirer and Perfecter, both of our faith and works.
>
> —John Wesley, "The Circumcision of the Heart"

James says this:

> My brothers and sisters, what good is it if people say they have faith but do nothing to show it? Claiming to have faith can't save anyone, can it? Imagine a brother or sister who is naked and never has enough food to eat. What if one of you said, "Go in peace! Stay warm! Have a nice meal!"? What good is it if you don't actually give them what their body needs? In the same way, faith is dead when it doesn't result in faithful activity.
>
> Someone might claim, "You have faith and I have action." But how can I see your faith apart from your actions? Instead, I'll show you my faith by putting it into practice in faithful action. It's good that you believe that God is one. Ha! Even the demons believe this, and they tremble with fear. Are you so slow? Do you need to be shown that faith without actions has no value at all? What about Abraham, our father? Wasn't he shown to be righteous through his actions when he offered his son Isaac on the altar? See, his faith was at work along with his actions. In fact, his faith was made complete by his faithful actions. So the scripture was fulfilled that says, *Abraham believed God, and God regarded him as righteous.* What is more, Abraham was called God's friend. So you see that a person is shown to be righteous through faithful actions and not through faith alone. In the same way, wasn't Rahab the prostitute shown to be righteous when she received the messengers as her guests and then sent them on by another road? As the lifeless body is dead, so faith without actions is dead. (James 2:14-26, CEB)

When doing good works, it is important to note that Methodists *do not* seek to earn God's favor by doing good. God has already shown favor on all people through the crucified and resurrected life of Jesus Christ. Methodists do good to live a full Christian life and to serve others as Christ exemplified, not to earn rewards.

A great place to start doing good works is to build relationships with communities and individuals within immediate social circles and discover the needs in our own backyard. Discovering what is needed and the opportunities to do good are as important as doing good itself. Encourage youth to take time on their own or with a smaller group of friends to look around their church, school, and community and listen for the needs out there. Good works can be done alone or with a group.

Share these ideas with the youth in your congregation:

- Create a list of the skills or assets you, as an individual, have (writing, technology, a car, and so forth). You can do good with the gifts you already have!
- Visit a local library or coffee shop and look at the community board of announcements. Discover new or up-and-coming places to serve or volunteer.
- Take a walking tour of all the churches within five miles of your home church. Look at the church buildings with an eye for building or maintenance projects or opportunities to serve groups in these churches.
- Schedule a meeting with a local school leader, and simply ask, "What could we do that would be good for your students or school?"
- Contact your local city government or parks and recreation office to find out existing programs that need volunteers.
- Sit in the worship space at your church and pray for guidance.
- Make a list of people whom you would consider your neighbors. For each of them, answer the question, "What could I do that would be good for them?"

Visiting Those Who Are Sick

Physical ailments can isolate people from communities, and sickness was prevalent in John Wesley's time. In fact, his Sermon 98, "On Visiting the Sick," quoted below, is completely about how and why to visit those who are sick. An important feature of this sermon is that John Wesley does not limit "the sick" to those who are bedridden but includes anyone who has any ailment. We also have the opportunity to serve those who are suffering emotionally and mentally. Of course, people in need of clinical care should see professionals with special training, but we don't have to be physicians or doctors to show that we care and meet some of the needs of a person who is suffering.

By the sick, I do not mean only those that keep their bed, or that are sick in the strictest sense. Rather I would include all such as are in a state of affliction, whether of mind or body; and that whether they are good or bad, whether they fear God or not.

"But is there need of visiting them in person? May we not relieve them at a distance? Does it not answer the same purpose if we send them help as if we carry it ourselves?" Many are so circumstanced that they cannot attend the sick in person; and where this is the real case it is undoubtedly sufficient for them to send help, being the only expedient they can use. But this is not properly visiting the sick; it is another thing. The word which we render visit, in its literal acceptation, means to look upon. And this, you well know, cannot be done unless you are present with them. To send them assistance is, therefore, entirely a different thing from visiting them. The former, then, ought to be done, but the latter not left undone.

John Wesley clearly identifies in-person contact and building relationships with the suffering, not just sending them assistance or checking in on them from a distance.

My wife, eighteen-month-old son, and I moved to Tennessee from Colorado in late 2012. Within the first two months of moving, our family came down with a virus that left us all with high fevers, vomiting, and several other symptoms (nasty symptoms!) that put us in an urgent care room receiving IV fluids to help us get hydrated and back on our feet. Besides the physical pain, we were feeling terrible because we no longer had family to check on our dog, to help bring us home, or to take care of us or our son and aid our recovery. We hadn't found a church home yet and were feeling alone, on top of feeling miserable. Fortunately, a now good friend from work, and a fellow United Methodist, met us at the hospital. It was good to have someone who cared enough not only to come see us at the hospital, but also to borrow keys to our house to take our dog for a walk. He made sure that we made it home after being discharged from the hospital and delivered a batch of excellent, homemade chicken noodle soup. Our ability to heal was helped so much by the support of this friend who through acts of compassion lived into this work of mercy.

People in our communities are hurting, and we can put ourselves, whether alone or with a group, in face-to-face situations with them.

Share these ideas with the youth in your congregation:

- Look over the prayer concern list in your church's bulletin to identify those suffering from illness. Find out who puts the list together, and ask how, in addition to your prayers, you can support those people.
- Identify children's hospitals in your area and connect with a volunteer group that works within those systems.
- Find retirement homes in your area that specialize in care for dementia or other chronic illnesses.

Visiting Those in Prison

Paul reminds us in Hebrews not to forget those in prison. We forget about those who are serving time in prison for many reasons: because we do not have a personal connection with them, because of fear, because they are out of sight and out of mind, and more. Maybe we even have an apathy or an unwillingness to forgive those who have committed crimes, yet we are called not to judge our neighbors but to love them as we love ourselves. Safety is also a consideration, but all places that house prisoners also employ guards and set up systems to allow visitation.

> Remember prisoners as if you were in prison with them, and people who are mistreated as if you were in their place.
>
> —Hebrews 13:3, CEB

Traditional prisons and juvenile detention centers are tremendous opportunities to serve and participate in works of mercy. The majority of those serving time in prison will be released at some point. Life sentences with no possibility of parole are few and far between, so the opportunity to visit and support those in prison means a better connection with them while they are behind bars, and the possibility of a better life once they rejoin society. Francis Asbury said, "My soul is more at rest from the tempter when I am busily employed," and this could very well be the case when visiting prisoners. We can be a part of helping busy the hands and minds of prisoners, introducing them to messages and a God they have not known or have forgotten. We can be in ministry with them by seeing them as people, not as actions or crimes. We can also continue to visit prisoners as they reenter society, helping them make connections, find work, and provide them a social network of support. Prisoners released from institutions can remain prisoners of systems that make life difficult for them.

Share these ideas with the youth in your congregation:

- A youth ministry blessed with committed singers, musicians, and directors was looking for opportunities to serve its community. A small, worship-leading group of young women met regularly during the year to rehearse. As they crafted their songs, they also made covenant relationships to support each other, and would hold their Covenant Discipleship group prior to rehearsal. During one Christmas season, the group was looking for places they could share their gift of song.

One person in the group knew of a women's prison within ten miles of their church. The group asked for the support of the choir director, talked with the prison administration, and was able to perform a Christmas worship service for the inmates. That initial outreach has now become two annual worship services, at Easter and Christmas. During the months between the services, the group and choir director remain in regular contact with some of the prisoners and leaders at the prison.

> My soul is more at rest from the tempter when I am busily employed.
>
> —FRANCIS ASBURY

- Locate prisons or incarceration facilities within a reasonable distance from your church home. Find out which ones are privately run and which ones are state run.
- Contact your local county court and find out what happens with adolescent detention in your area. Contact those facilities and find out if there are opportunities to visit. Even better, once there, ask the administrators of the facility what you can do to support the people there.
- Start a pen-pal connection between yourself or your Covenant Discipleship group and teens in detention facilities. Write monthly letters back and forth.

Feeding the Hungry

Today, hunger continues to be a worldwide issue, just as it was in John Wesley's day and time. Hunger can take many forms, and there are youth and children in every country who aren't sure where their next meal will come from. In the United States, this becomes particularly apparent during the summer months, when children and youth who receive free or reduced-cost lunches from the school they attend no longer are in class and can't count on that food. There are also many who have some food, but can afford only basic or processed foods that lack the nutritional value of fresh produce.

Several of Jesus' miracles involve food, and he would be among the first to say that the body, in addition to the soul, needs nourishment. After the feeding of the five thousand, people actually came seeking out more bread because of their bodily hunger. The miracle wasn't enough, they were hungry for more. Helping keep bodies nourished not only builds relationships and meets a need but also helps create the possibility for spiritual growth.

In the Gospel of John, Jesus has a conversation with a Samaritan woman, which was out of the ordinary for two reasons: (1) The Jewish people and the Samaritan people did not like each other at all, and (2) she was a woman! In the culture of the time, it was still uncommon for men to address women. In this conversation, Jesus asks the woman to give him a drink of water, and that simple action starts the conversation about the "living water" Jesus has to offer.

Jesus learned that the Pharisees had heard that he was making more disciples and baptizing more than John (although Jesus' disciples were baptizing, not Jesus himself). Therefore, he left Judea and went back to Galilee. Jesus had to go through Samaria. He came to a Samaritan city called Sychar, which was near the land Jacob had given to his son Joseph. Jacob's well was there. Jesus was tired from his journey, so he sat down at the well. It was about noon.

A Samaritan woman came to the well to draw water. Jesus said to her, "Give me some water to drink." His disciples had gone into the city to buy him some food.

The Samaritan woman asked, "Why do you, a Jewish man, ask for something to drink from me, a Samaritan woman?" (Jews and Samaritans didn't associate with each other.)

Jesus responded, "If you recognized God's gift and who is saying to you, 'Give me some water to drink,' you would be asking him and he would give you living water." The woman said to him, "Sir, you don't have a bucket and the well is deep. Where would you get this living water? You aren't greater than our father Jacob, are you? He gave this well to us, and he drank from it himself, as did his sons and his livestock."

Jesus answered, "Everyone who drinks this water will be thirsty again, but whoever drinks from the water that I will give will never be thirsty again. The water that I give will become in those who drink it a spring of water that bubbles up into eternal life."

The woman said to him, "Sir, give me this water, so that I will never be thirsty and will never need to come here to draw water!" (John 4:1-15, CEB)

Share these ideas with the youth in your congregation:

- Carry a nonperishable food item (like a granola bar) so that you always have something to give a hungry person.

- Locate local food pantries, soup kitchens, or other organizations that provide space and food but need volunteers to prepare and serve food. Join them and take time to eat with those who come for the food. Learn names and hear stories.
- Every Sunday that you have Communion, find a way to provide bread (or other food) to the hungry in your community.
- Find organizations that support single parents in your community, and see if you can prepare and pack a meal for a family, saving the parent time and money.
- Organize a peanut butter and jelly sandwich making in a city park.

Giving Generously to the Needs of Others

This work of mercy requires two things. First, the willingness to give and to give generously. So, how do we know if we are being generous? Some people measure generosity by a biblical tithe—giving back to God 10 percent of any money earned. Then everything given above that is considered to be generosity. Others measure generosity not only by what they give financially but also by the time, energy, or other things they give to others. After all, there are only twenty-four hours in a day no matter where we are from, so giving away some of our time to meet the needs of others is indeed generous!

> All worldly joys are less than that one joy of doing kindnesses.
>
> —John Wesley

The parable of the sower (Matt. 13:1-9) talks of a gardener walking along and dropping seeds everywhere. The gardener could be seen as careless, just tossing seeds all over the place and not placing them with care in orderly rows and in conditions that would guarantee a seed to sprout and bear fruit. The gardener is an example of generosity; he knows that there is much to give and that seeds will take root in even the most unlikely places. Likewise, we are called to give, and give generously of our time, talents, gifts, and service.

Second, this work of mercy requires seeing and realizing the needs of others. The culture we live in often encourages us to take care of ourselves. But if we spend our time asking only what do I need in life, how could anyone possibly give generously? We must grow beyond ourselves, get out of our normal routine, and try to see the world

> The believers devoted themselves to the apostles' teaching, to the community, to their shared meals, and to their prayers. A sense of awe came over everyone. God performed many wonders and signs through the apostles. All the believers were united and shared everything.
>
> —Acts 2:42-44, CEB

from someone else's point of view. Search and observe—seek and find—then give generously!

Sharing becomes a natural act in a life of discipleship. In the book of Acts, new converts to Christianity were so inspired by the disciples that they began to share, and share generously. Generous giving continues in today's church. For example, one worshiping community saw a need to support children and families going through treatments for major illnesses like cancer in their local hospital. One church member had the idea to visit the kids while they were in the hospital and give the children superhero capes to remind them how strong they were going through their treatments. The church member couldn't sew, didn't have money for supplies, and had no idea who to talk with at the hospital to get approval. The church member and pastor started talking, and sure enough, other members of the community gave their time, money, and talents to the idea. Now this church delivers capes to kids fighting cancer, and they are currently searching for other ways to support the families of those children.

Share these ideas with the youth in your congregation:

- Talk about what giving generously means.
- Make a list of the gifts, talents, and things that you could give.
- Look at the income you do have. What percentage do you currently give or donate? If it's 0 percent, start with 1 percent for a little while, then gradually increase what you give. Build donations into your personal budget.
- Spend time finding out where your giving can make the largest impact. Research places and people that you give to and find out how the donations that they receive are used.

Acts of JUSTICE

Acts of justice are public actions that reflect Jesus' command to love our neighbor as ourselves.

Seeking Justice

Methodists have a long history of seeking justice. Early Methodists advocated better working conditions for poorer groups of blue-collar laborers. Many of them took stands and action on slave trade, smuggling, and cruel treatment of prisoners. In fact, The United Methodist Church included a set of Social Principles (http://umc-gbcs.org/social -principles) and a Social Creed (http://www.umc.org/what-we-believe/our-social-creed) in the *Book of Discipline* that outline many groups in need of our voice as Christians. We see actions today in the UMC that continue to shine light on issues such as human trafficking, economic equality, prison reform, and even people's ability to get healthy food. Justice works hand in hand with compassion by addressing the systemic and structural forces that create inequality.

> Learn to do good. Seek justice; help the oppressed; defend the orphan; plead for the widow.
> —Isaiah 1:17, CEB

A well-known illustration that compares justice and compassion starts with a person standing by a river. The person suddenly notices a child floating down the river, keeping its head above water but struggling to swim to safety. The person of course shows compassion and jumps in the river to help pull the child to safety. As that child is drawn to safety, another is noticed in the river, and another, and another. People construct a small village to help these children, showing compassion. To seek justice is to walk farther upstream, undertaking the journey to discover what is causing these children to be in the river in the first place.

This image of the river, the children, the village, and the journey isn't perfect, but it does help us visualize how seeking justice considers systems that affect large numbers of people. It also helps us see that compassion is important; we do need to respond to the symptoms of systems that create inequality or unfairness. Yet, without seeking justice, the situation will not change and the village will pull kids from the river forever.

At a shopping mall, the custodial job is among the lowest-skilled positions and also the lowest paid. Being a mall custodian entails cleaning up after other people's messes, pushing a heavy cart of trash and cleaning supplies around for many hours, and standing on one's feet for extended periods. At one particular mall, the custodians were allowed a fifteen-minute break from work for every four hours on the job. It was their only opportunity to drink water. Rules from the management at the mall stated that the custodians could not use the water fountains in the mall (they were for shoppers) and they also could not carry water bottles during their cleaning rounds. A youth group who met for a Bible study in the food court of the mall got to know one of the custodians, because they saw him so regularly. They found out about the water issue and decided together that it was an issue of justice—that someone doing physical labor should be able to have water and stay hydrated as they needed, not just during breaks. The youth spoke with the management at the mall and the rules were changed to allow custodians to carry water bottles.

Share these ideas with the youth in your congregation:

- Pay attention to your gut feelings when something doesn't seem fair. If another person is being treated in a way that seems or feels unfair, ask questions about what is causing the unfairness.
- Practice empathy. Picture yourself living someone else's life, working their job, or being them in school and ask yourself, "What would make their life better?"

Ending Oppression and Discrimination

Over and over in scripture we are called to "be not afraid"—God seems to know that a frequent human response to something different or out of the ordinary is fear. The world is full of difference, on the surface. When fear drives people to focus on differences instead of remembering that we are all created in God's own image, people can begin to oppress and discriminate against their brothers and sisters. Fear is just one factor that can lead to oppression. Oppression happens when one person or group holds power over other people or groups and uses that power to limit or exert control. Discrimination can also be a response-based fear, but adds judgment to the picture to assign a value to a person's characteristics. Those perceived values, whether positive or negative, then affect how people treat one another.

> He has told you, human one, what is good and what the LORD requires from you: to do justice, embrace faithful love, and walk humbly with your God.
>
> —MICAH 6:8, CEB

As previously stated, Methodists have a long history of addressing oppression and discrimination. They even were present in the earliest parts of the Methodist movement. John Wesley saw his own church discriminating against field laborers. He found himself part of a church of elites, afraid to be in community with the margins of society. Today's world continues to be full of difference and full of fear. Imbalances of power also create the opportunity for people to oppress one another. People discriminate against each other, thinking that somehow something is less valuable about another person compared to themselves. Human trafficking, child labor, the sex trade, modern slavery, racism, brutality—the faces of oppression and discrimination continue to be strong forces that demand a thoughtful Christian response.

Oppression and discrimination become more powerful when mob mentality or groupthink becomes part of the equation. Encouraging societies or cultures to mature beyond oppressive or discriminatory behaviors is a long-view proposal, and as with any work of mercy, it starts with persons wanting to see a difference and starting with themselves.

Share these ideas with the youth in your congregation:

- Look around your community for people who are different from you. Make a list of the differences and similarities you have with your neighbors, classmates, and church friends.
- Find out what laws are in place in your community to prevent oppression and discrimination. Discover what and who are protected by law, and what or who aren't.

Addressing the Needs of Those Who Are Poor

In Matthew 25:25-40, Jesus plainly calls us to show grace and meet the needs of people who are poor. Paul reinforces the idea of meeting the needs of others in his letter to the Romans. Having the ability to address the needs of poor people springs from being in

> Love should be shown without pretending. Hate evil, and hold on to what is good. Love each other like the members of your family. Be the best at showing honor to each other. Don't hesitate to be enthusiastic—be on fire in the Spirit as you serve the Lord! Be happy in your hope, stand your ground when you're in trouble, and devote yourselves to prayer. Contribute to the needs of God's people, and welcome strangers into your home.
>
> —Romans 12:9-13, CEB

relationship with them, as noted earlier. Many communities become segregated by income. Homes of similar values are built together in neighborhoods, and often people who have the same income range buy those houses. Like Jesus, John Wesley would call us out if we were not in relationship with people who are poor.

Depending on the kind of poverty being experienced, the needs of poor people can change significantly between communities and contexts. That's why it is important for disciples to be out, actively engaged in the community and discovering the needs of people in their area who are poor. We can ask ourselves and other members of our church, how many poor people do we know? It's not a question of who do we know who serves the poor or where are the poor people in our community. The questions are: Who do we know in poverty? What are their names? Their stories? Their dreams and needs? Knowing leads to making a difference. When a statistic or label becomes a person with a name, it shifts our desire and ability to give generously.

Every Christmas in one congregation I know, along with the beautifully lit and ornamented church Christmas tree that sits outside the sanctuary, is a smaller tree covered in gift tags. A church member who is connected with a local thrift shop and storefront ministry has interviewed families in need to ask what they would like for Christmas. Some of the tags ask for toys, some of the tags ask for clothes. Others ask for books, art supplies, kitchen utensils. The tags are bunched together by family groups so that if a church member is going to purchase Christmas presents for a family in need, the member makes the commitment to purchase gifts for a whole family. Taking a family's worth of tags raises the member's awareness about the different needs even individuals within a family can have. A teenager's needs are different from a grade-schooler's, and both are different from their mother's. Often church members will look over the tree trying to find tags that mimic what their own families would ask for during the holiday season. When the gifts are purchased and brought back to the church, families leave knowing that they have met a need for a season—and are then invited to connect with different ministry opportunities throughout the year to continue meeting needs of people who are poor. One of the most popular options is connecting with another parent to support him or her in creating and managing a household budget.

As an act of justice, addressing the needs of people who are poor is larger than helping one family at a time. It is upstream discovery work. What is causing families like this to struggle financially? What is it about a group that increases the chances of them being poor in friends or poor in spirit?

Share these ideas with the youth in your congregation:

- Find ways to connect with people in your community who are poor. Define poverty broadly to include finances, friendships, or faith.
- Determine safe ways for youth to learn the names and stories of poor people in their communities.
- Consider what it is to be poor financially and also how to support people in ways that don't involve money.

Doing Works of Piety

Works of piety include acts of worship and devotion. Acts of worship are public and include participating in congregational worship and Communion, receiving and exploring God's Word together, and sharing faith. Acts of devotion are personal or private and include spending time with scripture, praying, and fasting.

Acts of WORSHIP

Acts of worship are public activities that reflect Jesus' command to love God with all our heart, soul, and mind.

Public Worship

John Wesley believed that authentic Christian worship was a central place to find God, Jesus, and the Holy Spirit, in an experiential way. Worship connects us to God's grace, assures us of God's love, and fills us with the joy of the Holy Spirit. It gives us the power to love God more fully and love our neighbors as ourselves. In his sermon "The Means of Grace," Wesley mentions the ministry of the Word, prayer, and Communion as elements of worship that connect us with the earliest followers of Christ. As we come to worship, we should be prepared to encounter God. God encounters can, of course, happen anywhere, but in worship we can expect to have our hearts warmed and our souls stirred. We can find plenty of scriptures about worship, and they all have something to do with coming together with others in praise. Joining together creates a special power and presence, especially when word and voice are given aloud as offerings!

The togetherness of worship is key here. Individual members of Covenant Discipleship groups can certainly worship in different places, but will often discover deeper levels of conversation when they worship together. Regularly and consistently worshiping creates opportunities for shared experiences. Picture a movie theater where people from all walks of life come together in one room for a set amount of time, expecting to hear and see a story, expecting to connect with characters who can reflect something about humanity, then all leaving when the show is over to discuss with friends the movie they just experienced together. Worship also brings together various people for a shared experience. Yet, disciples should not expect to be entertained. Rather, the expectation is that God is present in this space where I am putting myself! Singing together, praying aloud, and reading scripture together reinforce relationships among members of the body of Christ and also live into the kind of Christianity that John Wesley called a social religion. Christianity is meant to be experienced on a personal level, but also in community. Worship is a community's expression of their expectation to encounter God.

> Therefore, as God's choice, holy and loved, put on compassion, kindness, humility, gentleness, and patience. Be tolerant with each other and, if someone has a complaint against anyone, forgive each other. As the Lord forgave you, so also forgive each other. And over all these things put on love, which is the perfect bond of unity. The peace of Christ must control your hearts—a peace into which you were called in one body. And be thankful people. The word of Christ must live in you richly. Teach and warn each other with all wisdom by singing psalms, hymns, and spiritual songs. Sing to God with gratitude in your hearts. Whatever you do, whether in speech or action, do it all in the name of the Lord Jesus and give thanks to God the Father through him. (Col. 3:12-17, CEB)

Share these ideas with the youth in your congregation:

- Ask the pastor or church secretary for the order of worship for any or all worship services offered at your church. Look for the common elements between all the services.
- Try a different worship service than you usually go to.
- Make a commitment to worship alongside a Covenant Discipleship group for six weeks in a row.
- Look for ways to worship with the whole body of your church. If your church has a youth or contemporary service, invite someone who normally doesn't come to that service to attend with you. If you normally attend a worship

service separate or different from the traditional service, try attending the traditional service for a set amount of time.

Communion

The United Methodist Church recognizes two sacraments—and they are both things Jesus did during his time on earth: baptism and Communion. John Wesley would call these two sacraments "an outward sign of God's gift of inward grace." Instead of just a routine that shows commitment to a community, the sacraments are moments where we celebrate the grace given to us by God! Celebrating Communion in The United Methodist Church is a tradition linking us with the earliest Christians. John Wesley would say that as we take Communion, it is an opportunity for us to really feel the presence of Jesus. The taking of the cup and bread is sanctifying—an action that helps us feel God's grace as we walk the walk of a Christian life. Communion is important because it helps us respond to the immense love and grace God has shared with us.

Share these ideas with the youth in your congregation:

- Attend a Communion service at your church. Listen carefully to the words said by the pastor and the responses given by the people. Make a list of the questions you have about the "script" that leads up to Communion.
- Look for places and people in your church who don't have the opportunity to share in Communion. Find ways to bring Communion to them.
- Talk with your pastor about ways to take Communion out into the community.

Christian Conference

Covenant Discipleship is an expression of Christian conferencing. John Wesley, along with other early leaders of the Methodist movement, built their method around conferencing with each other—making an intentional space to share with each other about how their life was reflecting their faith.

> Every scripture is inspired by God and is useful for teaching, for showing mistakes, for correcting, and for training character, so that the person who belongs to God can be equipped to do everything that is good.
>
> —2 Timothy 3:16-17, CEB

Ministry of the Word

Reading scripture aloud in worship not only frames the message for the day but also creates a common reflection point for the worshiping congregation. John Wesley saw scripture as central to faith, so its inclusion in worship is natural. Friendships develop because of familiarity, and scripture is the same way. The more familiar we are with scripture, the better the chance that we'll develop a relationship with the Word.

Share these ideas with the youth in your congregation:

- Infuse scripture into various prayer practices during worship.
- Find opportunities to act out scriptures during worship.

Sharing Faith

Some people find that talking about what they believe with others can be difficult. Why? There are lots of potential reasons. Maybe people are worried that they'll be judged by others, maybe they are concerned they could lose a close friend, maybe people aren't sure enough about what they believe to talk about it clearly. People probably have lots of other reasons as well. Yet, there is something very important about sharing our faith with others, important enough that sharing faith is part of Jesus' last message to his disciples:

> Now the eleven disciples went to Galilee, to the mountain where Jesus told them to go. When they saw him, they worshipped him, but some doubted. Jesus came near and spoke to them, "I've received all authority in heaven and on earth. Therefore, go and make disciples of all nations, baptizing them in the name of the Father and of the Son and of the Holy Spirit, teaching them to obey everything that I've commanded you. Look, I myself will be with you every day until the end of this present age." (Matt. 28:16-20, CEB)

Jesus expects his disciples to go out and share with the world what they experienced and learned from Jesus. God is a relational being. God and Jesus both thrive in relationship with people—and every relationship starts with an introduction. Having a dynamic and growing faith is a great part of being a Methodist. We are asked to always look inward at our beliefs using scripture, reason, tradition, and experience. We expect our faith and beliefs to grow and change with time, just as our relationship with Jesus evolves. That means we can talk with others about what we believe—not to try to persuade someone else to join our viewpoint, but instead invite others to hear about our own experiences with God so that we can celebrate God together!

John Wesley saw sharing his faith with others as an integral part of his ministry. He believed that sharing was so important that he did not wait for pulpits and churches to welcome him but instead went out into fields and preached to anyone ready to hear.

One of John Wesley's well-known spiritual moments came about because someone shared their faith with him. In an evening society meeting, after John had a bad day, a group member was reading from Martin Luther's preface to the letter to the Romans. As the words were read, John said his heart felt "strangely warmed": "About a quarter before nine, while he was describing the change which God works in the heart through faith in Christ, I felt my heart strangely warmed. I

> I look on all the world as my parish; thus far I mean, that, in whatever part of it I am, I judge it meet, right, and my bounden duty, to declare unto all that are willing to hear, the glad tidings of salvation.
>
> —JOHN WESLEY, JOURNAL, JUNE 11, 1739

felt I did trust in Christ, Christ alone, for salvation; and an assurance was given me that He had taken away my sins, even mine, and saved me from the law of sin and death" (Journal, May 24, 1738).

We often share our faith in things that we find valuable or have made a difference in our lives. Faithful followers of tech companies (like Apple) will testify to the quality and usefulness of all things Apple and convince their friends to try them out. Faithful followers of apparel companies will wear only a certain brand of shoes, pants, shirts, or sunglasses and advertise to the world their loyalty to fashion icons. If we find our faith valuable, if we find that the relationship we are developing with God and Jesus makes a positive difference in our lives, it's worth sharing that with our friends and the world.

Share these ideas with the youth in your congregation:

- Write down one thing that you believe about God, Jesus, and the Holy Spirit. Share that list with a friend or family member and talk about why you believe that one thing.
- Write down one belief you've had for at least five years that hasn't changed. Discuss with another church member why it has stayed the same.

- Write down a belief that has changed or evolved in the last five years. Again, discuss it with a church member and why it changed.
- Take a walking tour of your community. It could be of your school, your neighborhood, and so forth. Where are the places and the people that could most benefit from hearing about God's grace and love?
- Say out loud to yourself, "I am a Christian. What does that mean?" See if you can tell your story of how you came to be a disciple to yourself before sharing the story with others.
- Create a collage of spiritual moments that have been especially meaningful or formative for your faith.
- Have your Covenant Discipleship group, or another group from church, meet in a public place for your discussion or check-in with each other.
- Read one of the famous creeds such as the Apostles' Creed. List out what you believe and don't believe. Discuss.
- When you are out doing good, make sure to always answer any question about why you are doing that activity.

Acts of DEVOTION

Acts of devotion are personal or private activities that reflect Jesus' command to love God with all our heart, soul, and mind.

Searching the Scriptures—Read, Meditate, Study

Since John Wesley saw scripture as central to a person's faith life, he encouraged familiarity with the Bible text itself. Scripture is accessible to all and is God's story of salvation, of making things new. Our response to God's saving work is our discipleship. So, reading scripture is a starting place, but we are called to reflect on the scriptures and study them. Discovering context can lead to new meanings and new readings.

Picture a Bible with print too small to read. A person pulls out a magnifying glass to make the text large enough to be seen. The curved glass that makes the letters larger also bends and changes the letters slightly, helping the person see the scripture in a new way. Meditating on and studying scripture helps create many different lenses through which we can understand scripture and begin to apply it to our lives.

Reading the Bible can be done alone, but an element of meditation and study is complemented by reading with a group and participating in a Bible study of some kind. Share these ideas with the youth in your congregation:

- Find a Bible app that outlines a plan for reading the entire Bible over the course of a year.
- Get a group of friends to do two Bible studies together—one that looks really interesting and is in line with your beliefs, and one that would not normally seem interesting or that challenges your beliefs. Be faithful in reading, studying, and discussing.
- Ask your family for their favorite passages of scripture, ask why they are favorites, and read the whole chapter or book that the scripture comes from.

> Rejoice always. Pray continually. Give thanks in every situation.
>
> —1 Thessalonians 5:16-18, CEB

Praying

Personal prayer can happen anywhere and any-time. Many of us grew up "saying grace" before meals, saying prayers before bedtime, or perhaps learning short rhyming prayers or the Lord's Prayer. The passage from 1 Thessalonians 5 encourages us to pray continually and with God in all things. It is a way to keep ourselves focused.

Sometimes we are not sure how to pray, or even what to pray for. We can pray for ourselves, for others, for the world. We can pray in lots of different ways, silently or aloud; while moving or still; with others or alone. Many excellent resources are available to help us develop meaningful prayer lives, and those resources often call the activities associated with prayer *practices*. Prayer is a way that we practice our faith, and we can practice many different ways of praying in order to discover what is most meaningful for us. Prayer centers us on our relationship with God, brings into focus the joys and sorrows on our minds, and can even be a way to be present in the lives of our friends and enemies.

Personal prayer can be grouped into four basic categories:

Adoration—prayers of worship and praise to God for being all that God is—Creator, Redeemer, Sustainer whom we love with all that we are

Confession—prayers that clear the air between us and God by admitting our imperfections and the places where we fall short of God's hope for us as people

Thanksgiving—prayers of thanks for the blessings in our lives and in the world

Supplication—prayers asking God to be present and to make changes in our own lives or in the lives of others

Prayer can be creative! There isn't just one way to pray, but many different ways that encourage the use of our minds, voices, bodies, gifts, talents, and skills. Search out different and creative ways to cultivate a meaningful prayer life. Remember, with each of the personal acts of devotion, getting into a regular habit makes their impact larger.

Share these ideas with the youth in your congregation:

- Search *Devozine* or *The Upper Room* websites for daily prayer devotionals. Use those devotionals to create a daily prayer opportunity for yourself.
- Start a journal of the things you pray about. Circle back to journal entries once a month to see how prayers have changed or how prayers have been answered.
- Research different prayer practices, such as Lectio Divina, body or breath prayers, and labyrinths. Try out a new prayer practice.

Before or after worship, start asking others the question, "What can I pray about for you?"

Fasting

Fasting has a strong scriptural foundation: Moses (Exod. 34:28), Elijah (1 Kings 19:8), Daniel (Dan. 9:3; 10:2-3); Paul (2 Cor. 11:27); and Jesus himself (Matt. 4:2) fasted so

> And when you fast, don't put on a sad face like the hypocrites. They distort their faces so people will know they are fasting. I assure you that they have their reward. When you fast, brush your hair and wash your face. Then you won't look like you are fasting to people, but only to your Father who is present in that secret place. Your Father who sees in secret will reward you.
>
> —Matthew 6:16-18, CEB

that they might draw closer to God. John Wesley fasted two days a week—Wednesdays and Fridays in his younger days—and continued to fast on Fridays even into his later life. Wesley found that fasting made more time for prayer and helped him give more generously to the needs of people who were poor.

Fasting traditionally means limiting how much food we eat or giving up certain kinds of food. However, a fast can be abstaining from anything that makes us devote time or energy away from living life as a disciple of Jesus Christ. People have fasted from TV, technology, dining out, and in other creative ways besides a traditional "no food" fast. The concept of fasting in Covenant Discipleship becomes more powerful because giving up one thing allows for generosity of that same thing. Cutting the size of a lunch one day a week will help us realize how much we consume other days of the week. It may also leave us hungrier than normal, reminding us to thank God for all that we have, or raise awareness of others who do not get regular meals. But fasting becomes transformational when we share what we did not consume because of our intentional fast. If we fast by cutting the size of our lunch in half on Friday, it is a powerful statement. It becomes transformational when we take the food from that Friday (or the money we saved) and give that to a person in need.

Share these ideas with the youth in your congregation:

- Choose one meal a week, and cut the amount you eat in half. Find a place or person to donate the normally used food (or money saved) toward.
- Research safe fasting practices and settle on a reasonable amount to try. Perhaps one day a month can be dedicated to juice fasts.
- Figure out what a fast from technology or social media looks like. Make your final posts, messages, or texts about your intentional time away from those places. Ask for prayers for those who don't have the benefit of these tools and platforms. Volunteer to teach elderly or other populations in need of technology training.
- Figure out the amount of money you spend on food not prepared in your home. Determine a percentage of that money that you could cut out of your budget and donate it to food kitchens or others in need.
- Take a food stamp challenge, living on the amount of money provided by government entities for free and reduced food lunches. Share the difference in money saved from a normal food budget and the food stamp budget with a local food pantry.

Healthy Living

John Wesley had plenty of thoughts on staying spiritually fit *and* physically fit. Wesley suggested that holiness had to do with *orthopraxis*—a word that means *how* we live is just as important as *what* we believe. It is important for us to do what we say we believe in.

Hypocrisy (not living out a belief) is a common criticism of Christians, and that could apply to healthy living as well. We often say that we believe eating a balanced diet, getting exercise, taking sabbath time, getting enough sleep, and avoiding gluttony are healthy things to do, but do we actually do them?

Wesley wrote and published a guidebook on healthy living in 1774 called the *Primitive Physick* that encouraged people to use preventive care and to avoid excess as a way to stay healthy. You'll be glad to know that exercise is included in the list of things to avoid in excess! (You'll also be glad to know that the cure for baldness he proposed was a miserable failure!) Wesley was all about balance, observing that a weak body could make for a weaker mind or spirit. The same kind of balance is called for in Covenant Discipleship. Intentionally balancing our faith actions, just like balancing the amount of physical exercise we do, or balancing the diets that we eat, creates better opportunities for us to live a balanced life centered on the cross. Here is a sampling of advice Wesley offers in *Primitive Physick*:

> The great rule of eating and drinking is, to suit the quality and quantity of the food to the strength of our digestion; to take always such a sort and such a measure of food as sits light and easy to the stomach.

> Water is the wholesomest of all drinks; quickens the appetite, and strengthens the digestion most.

> A due degree of exercise is indispensably necessary to health and long life.

> Walking is the best exercise for those who are able to bear it; riding for those who are not. The open air, when the weather is fair, contributes much to the benefit of exercise.

> Those who read or write much should learn to do it standing; otherwise it will impair their health.

The apostle Paul, in his letters, also addresses care of the physical body:

Or don't you know that your body is a temple of the Holy Spirit who is in you? Don't you know that you have the Holy Spirit from God, and you don't belong to yourselves? You have been bought and paid for, so honor God with your body. (1 Cor. 6:19-20, CEB)

So, brothers and sisters, because of God's mercies, I encourage you to present your bodies as a living sacrifice that is holy and pleasing to God. This is your appropriate priestly service. Don't be conformed to the patterns of this world, but be transformed by the renewing of your minds so that you can figure out what God's will is—what is good and pleasing and mature. (Rom. 12:1-2, CEB)

The concept of addiction is fairly new, but its consequences are far-reaching. People can become addicted, even to healthy things, and be thrown out of balance. Too much exercise and too much dieting can actually take away from a person's health. Also, addictions to drugs and alcohol are not healthy and damage the body. We need to take stock of our physical activity level, what we eat, and if we have addictions. Chances are that we'll find some ways we can become healthier. Keeping community and being in relationship with others is a healthy thing for people, as is having time on our own. We need to find places to connect with others while we take time for ourselves.

A young man had a roommate who drove him crazy. They had arguments all the time about who was taking whose food from the kitchen, who didn't clean up a mess. Anything that could be argued about was. This young man worked at a fast-food restaurant and had a pretty unhealthy diet. Because of that, coupled with lack of physical activity, he was overweight. After three months of arguing with the roommate, this young man decided to start running any time that he was frustrated. This occurred at least once or twice a week, and the run gave him time to process his anger in addition to being a healthy thing for his body. Fast-forward twelve months of running, and this young man had lost over 25 percent of his body weight and had to buy a smaller pair of shoes because even his feet lost weight!

Share these ideas with the youth in your congregation:

- Journal how much physical activity you have each day. Make a goal to get at least twenty to thirty minutes of activity every day.
- Discuss with friends what activities you really enjoy, especially team sports.

- Figure out a sabbath time for yourself to reflect on life, God, and rest from the busyness of life.
- Learn to cook. Cook for your family, friends, and others.

To help youth generate additional ideas for works of mercy and works of piety, see appendix A, "Bento Box Brainstorm and Challenge," and appendix B, "What's Your Frequency? Your DLC?"

Reflect, Don't Deflect

The ability to put beliefs into action starts with identifying a need. The previously listed ideas and stories all came about because people took the time find out their own needs for spiritual growth or put themselves in a situation where they could discover the needs of the neighbors and community. Works of piety can help us reflect upon those things that deserve attention in our own faith lives. We can set aside time on our own or in a Covenant Discipleship group to reflect upon our own needs, shortcomings of faith, and places where new seeds could grow. Likewise, we need to take time to put ourselves out into the community, then reflect upon where our presence and the presence of Christ will meet the needs of our neighbors.

As we go out into the community, we reflect the life and teachings of Christ to others, loving neighbor through works of mercy. We are image bearers of God, we carry the *imago dei,* and others will see the Holy Spirit working through us when we reflect the teaching and life of Jesus in our everyday lives. Let's not deflect the chance to share good news with our neighbors, ease their suffering, and connect with the Great Commandment. Let's not deflect the ability we have to make a difference, but let us do everyday things every day. Let us reflect the compassion, strength, virtue, and love of Christ by living in grace and doing works of piety and mercy regularly.

Works of Mercy

- Do good works
- Visit the sick
- Visit prisoners
- Feed the hungry
- Give generously to the needs of others

Personal

- Seek justice
- End oppression
- End discrimination
- Address the needs of the poor

Public

- Read, meditate, study scripture
- Pray
- Fast
- Live healthfully

Works of Piety

- Public worship
- Communion
- Ministry of the Word
- Christian conference
- Share faith

TL; DR Page

- The Bento Box Brainstorm and Challenge (appendix A) can help a participant or group brainstorm activities related to the means of grace (works of mercy and piety) that affect "me, we, or the world."
- The DLC (Do, Learn, Commit) activity (appendix B) can help potential participants in Covenant Discipleship realize what they are already doing and identify areas they would like to grow into.

- The good news: Each of us can be world changers by doing what we were designed to do—to be in relationship with other people and the rest of creation.
- The better news: Each of us can do many small things regularly (methodically), and over the course of time, those small things add up to a huge change, either in ourselves, in our communities, or in the world.

CHAPTER 4

Launching Covenant Discipleship Groups

By trying the ideas and activities suggested in the previous chapter, you can identify youth interested in the commitment level needed to participate in a Covenant Discipleship group. This chapter and a number of the appendixes outline a way forward, building a community of youth interested in the system and process of Covenant Discipleship. These suggestions are just that—suggestions. Building community and interest for Covenant Discipleship can happen in many different ways. The most important thing is starting somewhere. Simply by starting the conversation, you will find some youth who are naturally interested in the opportunity. Starting with just one young person or one group can be the seed that develops a culture of Covenant Discipleship in your context.

Starting

If you are using this resource in combination with either *Disciples Making Disciples* by Steven Manskar, the Covenant Discipleship resource for adults, or *Growing Everyday Disciples: Covenant Discipleship with Children* by Melanie Gordon, combine these

ideas and plans with the possibilities presented in those resources. Covenant Discipleship groups could become their own standalone group that youth participate in. They
could also be integrated into existing meetings such as youth groups, even taking place
before or after a regularly occurring program. Covenant Discipleship groups offer a way
to continue connections among members of a group that has gone through an experience together already, like a mission experience, in-depth Bible study, or even confirma-
tion or graduation.

When starting Covenant Discipleship, use these ground rules and allow the groups
to grow from there:

- Each group is no more than seven people.
- Each group has an identified guide who is part of the group. This person helps
  begin and close the time together. The guide can be an adult or youth.
- Each group meets once a week, regularly, with few breaks during the year.
- Each group writes their own covenant and provides copies of the covenant to each
  participant.
- Each group identifies their own starting and ending time, and really does start
  and end on time.
- Each group should share their covenant with the youth leader or minister.
- Each group can determine together with the youth leader if or when the group
  should cease meeting, split to form new groups, or invite new people into the
  group.

See appendix F, "Sample Timeline," for implementing Covenant Discipleship groups
with youth.

Who's Interested

Covenant Discipleship groups should be open to anyone, just like the historical class
meetings in early Methodism. Therefore, share information in lots of places and be in
conversation with all youth, as well as parents, connected to your local church and youth
ministry. Some youth will be interested in participating, others in becoming guides for
a Covenant Discipleship group, and some of course will look at the commitment level
and decide that Covenant Discipleship is not for them. Don't miss the opportunity to

help youth know about Covenant Discipleship and the opportunity it presents for them to live out their faith in a real and tangible way.

Individual conversations can build up buy in for Covenant Discipleship, but also prepare to offer informational meetings that bring together interested youth and parents. Also, present your concepts and plans to other church staff and lay leaders. They may be helpful in identifying times and spaces that groups could meet if they elect to meet at church.

Once interested people are identified, a youth leader will have an idea of the number of guides needed.

Identifying Guides

Mutual accountability in Covenant Discipleship groups means that the youth leader removes himself or herself from direct control of and influence over the groups. In reality, for a youth leader to be an active participant in multiple groups would be impossible. Instead, the youth leader becomes the facilitator and organizer of the system and not a participant in the groups. The term *guides* is used for Covenant Discipleship with youth. These individuals would be called class leaders in a traditional Covenant Discipleship system. Refer to Steve Manskar's adult Covenant Discipleship resource *Disciples Making Disciples* for further information on the training of class leaders.

With the youth leader organizing and facilitating the system, a youth or adult participant must step up and be willing to become a guide for a group. The role of a guide is not to have the correct answers or be the leader of the group but rather to guide the group to make sure they start and end on time and to keep the conversation moving. Covenant Discipleship groups can be youth only or mixed age. If an adult is involved as a participant in the group, he or she should not always be the default guide. Youth should have the opportunity to fill those roles.

Youth or adult volunteers that make suitable guides have one or more of the following characteristics:

- punctual
- organized
- committed
- positive
- caring

- compassionate
- collaborative
- self-aware
- supportive
- listens well

Serving as a guide for a Covenant Discipleship group does not mean an increased workload during the week beyond the covenant the group sets in place. A guide's two central responsibilities are to encourage everyone to attend the standard meeting time each week and to help the gathering start and end on time.

Identify at least two potential guides for each Covenant Discipleship group you hope to start. Once guides are identified, you can start planning the first meeting and create groups of seven or fewer to begin Covenant Discipleship processes.

The First Gathering

An ideal way to launch the process is with a gathering that brings together everyone interested in Covenant Discipleship. At this event a youth leader, or potentially a few guides, will lead people through condensed versions of this resource in order to help all participants start from the same place regarding their familiarity with Covenant Discipleship.

This gathering should at least include the following:

- The biblical and historical underpinnings of Covenant Discipleship
- A review of the works of piety and mercy and a call to explore living a balanced life of faith
- An overview of the format of group meetings and the time commitment involved; this includes the designed time frames that groups are set to run
- Commitments from those interested in joining a group
- Sharing how Covenant Discipleship feeds into the youth ministry and whole life of the church
- Modeling what healthy discussion and sharing look like in a Covenant Discipleship group setting

At the end of this gathering, the youth leader and guides can take the commitments from individuals, arrange them in Covenant Discipleship groups, inform participants who they are grouped with, and help them arrange to begin meeting in their groups of seven or fewer.

Individual Covenant Discipleship groups should write their covenant together once the groups are formed by the youth leader and guides.

Just like covenants, the time frames for group meetings are flexible and subject to the choices of the youth leader and participants. Some Covenant Discipleship groups can meet with no specific end date in mind. Others may meet for a set period, such as a year, a school year, or even as short as four months at a time. Each group sets their meeting day and time, preferably once a week, and members faithfully show up to share about their week.

Appendix D, "First Gathering Invitation," provides an example of what information to include in the invitation.

See appendix E, "Organizing and Assigning Groups," for a table to use as you identify participants, the groups to which they're assigned, and where and when the groups meet.

Writing Covenants

Writing a covenant may be a new experience for participants in Covenant Discipleship groups, and it should be the first thing a new group does. The first gathering may create a buzz and excitement to get started, and that excitement must translate into the creation of the covenant to which a group will hold each other accountable. This means that the thoughtful preparation of a covenant addressing how participants will live out a balanced life of discipleship is key to the success of a group. Let's go back to the metaphor from Hebrews 12:1 of running the race "set before us." Running a race takes some preparation, stretching, getting the body ready, perhaps eating the right foods, and getting the right clothing together. The Covenant Discipleship race isn't a sprint, it is a marathon. It's a long-game process of faith development, and the more time given to preparation, often the stronger the results.

Covenants usually have three basic parts: the preamble, the clauses, and the conclusion.

Preamble:

- Explains why the group is making a covenant
- States what commitments the group is making to each other
- Reminds participants that the commitments are guides, not regulations
- Includes a reminder of grace at work in the group and its actions
- Makes a shared statement of faith in Christ
- Is read aloud, together, at the start of each Covenant Discipleship meeting

Clauses:

- Spell out the goals for participants
- State how participants will individually live out the teachings of Christ through works of mercy and works of piety
- Create balanced actions by addressing personal and public acts of compassion, justice, devotion, and worship
- Are as simple and as specific as possible
- Are things that everyone in the group is willing and able to do
- Should not number any more than eight to ten

Conclusion:

- Briefly reaffirms the preamble of the covenant
- Emphasizes grace as well as dynamic or developing faith
- Reminds participants of their connection to God, Jesus, the Holy Spirit, and each other
- Is read aloud, together, as a closing to each Covenant Discipleship meeting

Finally, covenants can develop and evolve over time. If a group continues to meet for a longer period (more than six months), revisiting and updating the covenant is appropriate. Perhaps the activities done (acts of compassion, justice, worship, and devotion) have shone a light on expressions of faith that are missing and could be included or have helped the group discover needs in the community not currently being met. If a new person joins the group, it is an excellent opportunity to review and refresh the covenant.

Once a covenant is finalized, the Covenant Discipleship group reads the covenant aloud together and signs it.

- Each participant gets a copy of the covenant. Electronic, print, or even a picture is great.
- The youth leader gets a copy of the covenant.
- If the group is meeting regularly at a space in the church, a copy of the covenant could be kept on hand to pull out when the group meets.
- Refer to appendix C, "Covenant Examples," for help with developing covenants.
- Participants can review covenants from other groups, taking and adapting bits and pieces that feel the most relevant and needed for their context.

- Participants can start by creating lists of behaviors they feel would most benefit them as disciples.
- Participants can also always refer back to the General Rule of Discipleship and create clauses that will most easily help them show their love for God and love of neighbor.
- For easy math, participants can create either four or eight clauses. Four clauses would be one action in each category of compassion, justice, devotion, and worship. Eight clauses would make two actions in each category.

Once a group has been organized and they have created their covenant, away they go to transform themselves and the world! A group has started up, created and signed their covenant, and knows how long they'll be meeting; now it's time for the group to live into the covenant, keeping their faith active and growing.

Full Participation

Organized youth leaders will help their guides and participants stay engaged, doing the everyday things, every day, that are outlined in the covenants. The youth leader can do so by checking in regularly with anyone participating in a Covenant Discipleship group and asking questions related to the group's covenant.

For a participant, full participation in Covenant Discipleship means

- regularly joining the group for face-to-face meetings,
- listening and sharing during the meetings,
- looking for opportunities during the week to intentionally do the actions listed in the group's covenant, and
- holding other group members in prayer during the week.

Appendix G, "Model Behavior in Covenant Discipleship Groups," can be distributed to and reviewed by a group periodically.

Checking In

Covenant Discipleship participants meet to check in with each other, asking, "How is it with your soul?" and, as John Wesley phrased it, "How is your doing?" In other words, are participants doing the things they promised each other and how are they showing their love of God and neighbor?

When participants ask these questions in the group, going line by line through the covenant's clauses, it is important for them to be active listeners. Listening to fellow disciples on the same journey will help them ask questions, spark ideas in their own minds, and provide things that they can pray about during the week.

Likewise, it is important for participants to feel comfortable enough to share more than one-word or one-sentence answers. Let's say that one of a group's clauses is to "pray for enemies." A group of five could answer that question in five seconds by simply taking turns saying, "Yes, I did that this week," but that doesn't answer the question, how is your doing? Knowing if someone did pray for an enemy is fine, but understanding how they prayed for that enemy, how that person came to be an enemy, how the situation changed because of prayer, those are the stories that develop mutual support and accountability in the group. The youth leader and guide can encourage participants to share more than simple yes and no answers and to explore the *how* side of the clauses of a group's covenant.

It is okay for group members not to do everything in the covenant every week. John Wesley understood that people were not perfect and that our lives are a journey toward perfection. Perhaps they're journeys that can never be completed, but we can take each day and do it better than the last. A life of discipleship isn't about trying to do yesterday better, but trying to do today and tomorrow better. A Covenant Discipleship group is a space safe enough for a participant to share when they haven't done something or have fallen short of their desire to become a more faithful disciple.

Group guides can check in on other participants from their group between face-to-face meetings if they wish, but it's not required. Youth leaders should check in on the guides on a regular basis to ensure that they are happy with how their group dynamic is evolving.

Modeling Discipleship

Covenant Discipleship groups can be reinforced by sharing their experiences with others. Participants in Covenant Discipleship have the opportunity to make more disciples by inviting them to try out Covenant Discipleship for themselves. The youth leader and guides can help participants recognize that they are acting in ways that others could emulate. Disciples make more disciples, and members of Covenant Discipleship groups can be encouraged to invite other youth to try out groups, even without them attending a formalized first gathering.

Similarly, youth participating in Covenant Discipleship groups will tell amazing stories about their experiences, which a youth leader could share with other church leaders and the congregation. By regularly checking in with groups, a youth leader will have plenty to share about how their youth are developing into world-changing disciples and learning to love God and neighbor. Be intentional about sharing the growth and challenges coming out of Covenant Discipleship.

If the whole church is using Covenant Discipleship groups with multiple age groups, create opportunities to gather guides or participants from different groups to share what is working in their groups.

Evaluating Effectiveness

Evaluation of Covenant Discipleship is important from a leader's standpoint. The process and system of Covenant Discipleship does require organization, time, and perhaps even a small budget in order to launch it and for it to become a part of youth ministry. Traditional metrics the church uses are important to track, such as overall attendance or number of youth involved in small groups. However, there are also a few other indicators youth leaders can pay attention to as a way of tracking the success of Covenant Discipleship. Appendix H offers several evaluation tools for you to use.

"Who Do You Say That I Am?"

In Mark 8, Jesus asks one of his most important questions of the disciples: "Who do you say that I am?" (verse 9). A life of discipleship is meant to help us answer that personal question. We are not to rely on what others tell us about the person, the divinity, the life of Christ. We are meant to experience him through our actions, especially with those in need. By intentionally putting ourselves in places where we are likely to see the face of Jesus, with those in need on the margins of society, we will come to clearer answers about who Jesus is. Our answers need not match, but a basic understanding of who

Christ is will appear in the preamble of a group's covenant. Therefore, one method of tracking effectiveness in Covenant Discipleship is to find out how youth participants' understanding of Jesus develops and changes over time.

Every six months you, as a youth leader, could provide participants with a set of statements about Jesus, designed to measure Christology, or familiarity with Jesus' teachings or actions in human life. Ask participants to rank their agreement or disagreement with the statements and answer the question, "Who do you say Jesus is?" Tracking the changes in those answers will undoubtedly show a change in spiritual maturity.

In doing this, a youth leader will track any increased familiarity with the teachings and life of Jesus, discover how many opportunities a youth has to live out those teachings, and even measure the chances to engage "the least of these" because of a participant's involvement in Covenant Discipleship.

"How Is It with Your Soul?"

At the earliest Methodist meetings, John Wesley asked the question: "How is it with your soul?" Youth leaders can ask that same question to measure relative changes in attitudes or activity levels. Each participant in Covenant Discipleship will come to the group with a different set of experiences, understandings, and activity levels. The goal of mutual accountability is to grow in faith and intentional activities related to discipleship. Once a group's covenant is set, a youth leader could take the clauses and, at the beginning of the group, have all participants rate how important they think the action is to their own faith development, how important the act is to the community, and how often they do the act. Then, after a set period of time (such as six weeks or six months), the youth leader could provide the same assessment to see how the participants' attitudes and activity levels have changed. Demonstrating a growth toward spiritual maturity through intentional discipleship is a "win" in Covenant Discipleship.

"Where Are You Seeing God?"

The question "Where are you seeing God?" seems to be a favorite among mission and service expeditions, and the question can also be used to assess how effective a group is living into their covenant. Being in a mutually accountable group increases the relational surface area a youth has. The person is more frequently in touch with the other participants in the group while being more frequently engaged with the community. Since Christianity is a social religion, per John Wesley, measuring how many opportunities a young person has to be in community because of Covenant Discipleship is a valid measure. The youth leader could look at chances to develop relationships within a peer group or community as a measure of success in Covenant Discipleship.

Another measure of effectiveness is how many more opportunities for cultural exegesis happen because of a youth's involvement in Covenant Discipleship. By cultural *exegesis*, I mean seeing God and finding meaning in the culture we are surrounded by and making sense of the culture we live in through a Christian perspective. God is in all things, and culture is not the enemy; God is there too somewhere. A youth leader could ask youth how they have engaged culture and shared discussions of faith in their community.

Signals for Change

Sometimes, groups run their course through a natural lifecycle. Sometimes, groups never gel and fall apart because of weak connections. Sometimes unhealthy group dynamics arise and pop the safety bubble required for growth and authenticity. The youth leader and guides should be on the lookout for symptoms in groups that may require the youth leader to step in and create change. Symptoms that youth leaders and guides can observe that may signal the need for change include these:

- Attendance problems
- Incomplete covenants
- Failure to progress through the covenant or more regularly do the actions in the clauses
- Exceptionally short group meetings
- One-word or one-sentence answers
- Unhealthy group dynamics

Future Adaptation

Before launching a Covenant Discipleship effort as a part of youth ministry, the youth leader and church will have created a plan, a timeline, (hopefully!) a budget, and measures of effectiveness. The youth leader and guides should be faithful in tracking attendance and effectiveness, looking for ways to improve disciples' experiences in these covenant groups.

Perhaps a youth leader will discover that reorganizing participants into new groups every four to six months helps develop new relationships and keeps the expressions of faith more fresh and relevant. Perhaps an original plan to have the groups be youth only changes and they become intergenerational groups. Adapting the structure and system of Covenant Discipleship is an important job of the youth leader as an organizer. The leader's work helps create the most chances for beneficial experiences and spiritual development.

Finally, a reminder: It is indeed disciples who make other disciples. Testimonies and stories from those participating in Covenant Discipleship groups are powerful pieces to share with the church as a whole and with other prospective participants. Collecting these stories and having them ready to share will benefit youth leaders as they develop their ministry plan for the long term.

TL; DR Page

- Before launching into Covenant Discipleship groups and covenants, a plan to introduce and integrate Covenant Discipleship into youth ministry and the ministry of the whole church is needed. A youth leader is the logical person to initiate the plan.
- A youth leader's duty is to help organize the system and process, not to participate in every group.
- General group guidelines:
  - Each group has no more than seven people.
  - Each group has an identified guide who is part of the group, who helps begin and close the time together. The guide can be an adult or youth.
  - Each group meets once a week, regularly, with very few breaks during the year.
  - Each group writes their own covenant and provides copies of the covenant to each participant.
  - Each group identifies their own starting and ending time, and really does start and end on time.
  - Groups should share their covenants with the youth leader or minister.
  - Groups can determine together with the youth leader if or when the group should cease meeting, split to form new groups, or invite new people into the group.
- Hosting a "first gathering" is a good way to get all potential participants on the same page.

- The youth leader and other leaders of the church can be instrumental in helping youth write their own covenants for their groups. Creating a covenant may be a new exercise for youth, so allowing enough time to create a quality covenant is an important part of preparation.
- Youth leaders can measure the effectiveness of Covenant Discipleship groups by
  - tracking total participants involved in groups;
  - tracking participants' ability to answer the question, "Who do you say that I am?" (Mark 8:29);
  - tracking relative changes to attitudes or faith-interactive activity levels; and
  - collecting stories about where God was seen, Jesus was interacted with, or the Holy Spirit was felt.
- Sometimes original plans must change, and that's okay. Some groups won't click and work out, but others will be incredibly strong. An organized youth leader can stay in touch with guides and groups to know when change is needed.
- The good news: Covenant Discipleship groups are adaptable to a wide range of settings, require little funding, and can be measured as effective in many different ways.
- The better news: Covenant Discipleship groups increase the relational surface area of participants and therefore increase the opportunities of the youth leader and the church to interact with and engage their surrounding community.

APPENDIX A

Bento Box Brainstorm and Challenge

To help create ideas for the acts of compassion, devotion, justice, and worship, try the bento box challenge and compare ideas with others in your Covenant Discipleship group.

The acts of compassion, justice, devotion, and worship that members of a Covenant Discipleship group participate in can take an infinite number of forms. You can customize how you do each action by focusing on who the action is designed to affect.

Bento Box Brainstorm

In the left-hand column of the Idea Table below are all of the means of grace discussed in this resource, followed by three columns marked "Me," "We," and "World," according to the intended beneficiary of the action.

"Me" means the action you choose will be focused internally on your own spiritual growth.

"We" means the action you choose will be focused on your local church or youth group, benefitting people you are connected with through church or youth group.

"World" means the action you choose will be focused on any community outside your church, benefitting anyone who is currently outside your local church.

For each action on the left, come up with some ideas that you (or your Covenant Discipleship group) could do in the next six weeks. You don't have to come up with an activity for absolutely every line, but trying to fill out the whole table will give you a challenge, and a great appreciation for how you can customize the actions your Covenant Discipleship group includes in their commitments.

Idea Table

Action	Me	We	World
Personal Mercy (Compassion)			
Do good works			
Visit the sick			
Visit prisoners			
Feed the hungry			
Give generously to the needs of others			
Public Mercy (Justice)			
Seek justice			
End oppression			
End discrimination			
Address the needs of the poor			
Personal Piety (Devotion)			
Read, meditate on, study scripture			
Pray			
Fast			
Live healthfully			
Public Piety (Worship)			
Worship			
Communion			
Christian conference			
Bible study			
Share faith			

Bento Box Challenge

After completing the Idea Table, insert your ideas from the table in the bento box below to create a balanced set of commitments to live into your covenant. As you do actions for the benefit of the community and world, you will personally benefit as well.

Finding ways to do acts of devotion, worship, compassion, and justice that benefit different groups of people in addition to yourself is central to Covenant Discipleship.

Compassion for my community:	Compassion for the world:		Justice for my community:	Justice for the world:
Devotion for my community:	Devotion for the world:		Worship for my community:	Worship for the world:

What's Your Frequency? Your DLC?

T he DLC (Do, Learn, Commit) sheet below offers Covenant Discipleship groups a way to start talking about the means of grace (works of mercy and works of piety).

Do, Learn, Commit—DLC

The actions listed are both private and public. Refer to page 59 to find out which actions you can do by yourself and which actions you must do in community with others.

1. How often do you already **do** the means of grace as a disciple of Jesus Christ? *Mark the boxes in the table below with a **D** for every activity you already **do**.*

2. What means of grace would you like to **learn** more about? *Mark the boxes in the table below with an **L** for every activity you'd like to **learn** more about.*

3. What new means of grace would you **commit** to doing for the next six weeks? *Mark the boxes in the table below with a **C** for every new activity you will **commit** to.*

Works of Piety	Every Day	Once a Week +	Once in Two Weeks +	Once a Month	Almost Never
Read, meditate on, study scripture					
Pray					
Fast					
Live healthfully					
Worship					
Communion					
Christian conference					
Bible study					
Share faith					

Works of Mercy	Every Day	Once a Week +	Once in Two Weeks +	Once a Month	Almost Never
Do good works					
Visit the sick					
Visit prisoners					
Feed the hungry					
Give generously					
Seek justice					
End oppression					
End discrimination					
Address needs of the poor					

What one means of grace would make the biggest difference in your life if you did it more regularly?

What one means of grace would make the biggest difference in your church or local community if it was done more regularly?

APPENDIX C

Covenant Examples

Preambles

We are disciples of Jesus Christ. God intends to save us from sin and for us to live lives of love to God and neighbor. God has called us and the Spirit has empowered us to be witnesses of God's kingdom and to grow in holiness all the days of our lives. We commit ourselves to use our time, skills, resources, and strength to love and serve God, neighbor, and creation, trusting God's power through these means to make us holy.

We know that Jesus Christ died for us. We are called by God to be disciples of Jesus. We practice being disciples together so we can together experience God's love, forgiveness, guidance, and strength. Following the Holy Spirit, we will show compassion, justice, worship, and devotion.

Jesus, we want to be more like you. Every day is filled with opportunities to meet you on the margins. God and the Holy Spirit call us out, making our actions intentional.

Our time, energy, and talents are dedicated to showing our love for you and for our neighbors.

We aren't perfect, but we're getting better every day. Jesus' life set a pattern we try to follow with our minds and hearts. We are partners in grace, living out the Great Commandment in everything we do. We are everyday people called to be more like Christ, and we promise each other that God will get the best we have to offer.

Clauses

In addition to the suggestions that follow, use the Idea Table on page 77 to come up with ideas for clauses.

Take the Jerusalem cross image and print or draw it on a large sheet of paper. Set it on a table in the middle of a group. Have each person write ideas for each of the four categories (compassion, justice, devotion, worship) on scraps of paper and place them in the appropriate category on the sheet. Discuss, combine, and select clauses from these piles.

Here are a few ideas to start with:

Compassion

- Find chances to serve others in our community (home, church, school, teams, and so forth).
- Show our thanks.
- Participate in a service or volunteer project organized by someone else.
- Give time to a local nonprofit.
- Do a random act of kindness for a stranger.

Justice

- Be honest and kind.
- Speak out against prejudice in any form that we encounter.
- Be as eco-friendly as possible.
- Participate in conversations about culture and faith.
- Break stereotypes and develop friendships.
- Encourage forgiveness.

Devotion

- Pray for the members of my Covenant Discipleship group.
- Read scripture every day.
- Discover and try a new prayer practice.
- Exercise twice a week and get enough rest.
- Be at my Covenant Discipleship group.
- Say a pray of thanks before everything I eat.

Worship

- Worship with my community.
- Find ways to give my money, time, and talents.
- Be a part of Communion as often as possible.
- Read a devotional that I've never read before.
- Bring a friend to worship or another church activity.

Conclusions

Open our eyes to your presence, God, that we can see you in the expected and unexpected places, and in the faces of our brothers and sisters in Christ. Open our ears to your will, that we can hear you calling us forth. Open our hearts and hands in mercy, so that we may receive mercy when we fail. Amen.

These words are our own, and the actions and spirit behind our devotion is for you, O God. Help our hands, feet, hearts, hands, and minds love you and love neighbor while we do everyday things every day. Amen.

Lord, keep our focus on loving you and loving our neighbors. Be with us when we go out looking for Jesus and the opportunities to live out his teachings. Remember us as we remember you in all that we do. Help us to stay centered on the cross, even as we reach out to the very margins of society. Amen.

Two Versions of John Wesley's Covenant Prayer

Traditional (as used in the Book of Offices of the British Methodist Church, 1936):
     I am no longer my own, but thine.
     Put me to what thou wilt, rank me with whom thou wilt.

Put me to doing, put me to suffering.
Let me be employed for thee or laid aside for thee,
exalted for thee or brought low for thee.
Let me be full, let me be empty.
Let me have all things, let me have nothing.
I freely and heartily yield all things to thy pleasure and disposal.
And now, O glorious and blessed God, Father, Son and Holy Spirit,
thou art mine, and I am thine.
So be it.
And the covenant which I have made on earth,
let it be ratified in heaven.
Amen.

Modern (the Methodist Church in Britain):
I am no longer my own, but yours.
Put me to what you will, rank me with whom you will;
put me to doing, put me to suffering;
let me be employed for you, or laid aside for you,
exalted for you, or brought low for you;
let me be full,
let me be empty,
let me have all things,
let me have nothing:
I freely and wholeheartedly yield all things
to your pleasure and disposal.
And now, glorious and blessed God,
Father, Son and Holy Spirit,
you are mine and I am yours. So be it.
And the covenant now made on earth, let it be ratified in heaven.
Amen.

APPENDIX D

First Gathering Invitation

Hey!

Ever felt like there was more you could do to both figure out and practice your faith? We are exploring something called Covenant Discipleship as an opportunity for our church to learn more about each other and God. We'd love for you to check out what we've put together as a new and different way for you to experience God.

We'll have a quick meeting in _____ on _____. Joining us for this first gathering doesn't mean you have to become a covenant disciple; it's just a chance to learn a little bit more and see if it's the right fit for you. We really value intentional community, caring for one another and being honest in our faith.

I hope that you'll take the time to find out if Covenant Discipleship is the right adventure for you. If you want to join our first gathering, here's what you need to do:

- Contact me at _____ and say "I'm in!" I'll send you a few items to look over before the meeting starts.
- Join our first gathering at _____ (date, time, place).

Organizing and Assigning Groups Table

Name	Age	Gender	Guide or Class Leader	Meeting Time and Place

Sample Timeline

Three months before group launch:

- Discuss Covenant Discipleship process with church and youth leadership in the church.
- Determine age levels and format.
  - Single age? Mixed age? Adult participants included?
  - Single gender?
  - Independent groups? Will they meet on their own, in addition to anything else currently offered as a part of youth ministry?
  - Integrated groups? Will they meet as a part of, or in a related way, to something else currently offered in youth ministry?
  - Continuation groups? Will they meet as a way of continuing to build community after youth have fulfilled a short-term commitment?
  - Time frame? Form groups and allow them to meet indefinitely? Form groups for one year, nine months, six months, four months? How often will the groups be rearranged?
  - Budget? Will there be any cost associated with the launch of Covenant Discipleship groups? With recruiting or training guides? Meetings?

- Begin recruitment and training of guides (class leaders).
  - Identify potential guides and participants.
  - Share information about Covenant Discipleship among the whole church.
  - Provide guides with material to inform them about the benefits of Covenant Discipleship and the role of the guide.

Two months before group launch:

- Receive commitments from guides.
- Bring guides together to perform a brief training, to share the structure of the groups and time frame during which they will meet, to practice writing covenants, and to discuss healthy group dynamics.
- Begin advertising and sharing information about the groups in the best places to reach the congregation.
- Follow congregation approval processes (if in place) for creating new groups or ministries.
- Determine how effectiveness of groups will be measured.

One month before group launch:

- Host the "first gathering" informational meeting. Attendees are invited to bring parents, all information is shared, and the opportunity to commit to joining a group is offered.
- Create a system to track covenants and group attendance and to support guides.
- Form groups with assigned leaders.

Two weeks before group launch:

- Share contact information for participants assigned to a guide.
- Groups identify the time and day of the week for their regular meeting.
- Guides contact their groups to set the group's first meeting time and place

One week before group launch:

- Pray over guides and introduce them to the congregation.
- Confirm groups and participants. Make a list of any and all group meeting times and places.
- Check in with guides. Provide any resources they require prior to launch.

Group launch:

- Groups begin meetings.
- First meeting includes time for introductions (if needed) and writing of covenant. (Covenants can sometimes take two or three meetings to develop as a group. If a group gets stuck on creating their covenant, offer guidance.)
- Provide an evaluation tool for the group to complete at the beginning of their first meeting.
- Groups continue to meet weekly.
- Check in with guides every two weeks to see how things are going.

One month after group launch:

- Confirm that attendance remains steady.
- Confirm that group(s) have realistic and complete covenants.
- Provide groups with whatever evaluation tool is used to measure success. Have them complete evaluation tool.
- Collect initial group responses (with names).
- Share launch information with church and youth leadership.

Three months after group launch:

- Confirm that attendance remains steady.
- Ask group(s) if their covenants need updating after trying to live them out for twelve weeks.
- Determine if original timeline and plan are serving the needs of the participants. Begin reorganizing if needed.
- Issue follow-up evaluation tool, comparing results between this round and first round.
- Share results with participants, guides, and church and youth leadership.
- Begin process of reorganizing groups if needed, determining if groups need to split or if others should be invited to join, if new groups should be started, and so forth.
- Repeat this step at six months, or return to suggestions for "group launch" above.

Model Behavior in Covenant Discipleship Groups

Guides start and end meetings on time. The preamble and conclusion of the covenant are read aloud as a group.

Participants arrive on time, willingly repeat the covenant aloud together, and freely share what or what was not accomplished during the previous week.

All participants listen and respond without judgment, but with an attitude of care and support.

Participants have tried during the week to live into the covenant they set for themselves.

Participants do not interrupt each other, but listen actively and respond appropriately.

Participants are honest with themselves and each other.

Participants share briefly but deeply, respecting the time of their fellow disciples and the group.

Guides keep the discussion on track, referring back to the covenant when needed.

All participants, including the guide, bring a copy of their covenant to each meeting.

Participants inform others of meetings they cannot attend as soon as they know.

A spirit of grace and forgiveness permeates the time together.

Guides and participants freely share with the youth leader in addition to their group.

Participants and guides find creative ways to stay in touch with each other between weekly meetings or in lieu of weekly meetings.

Signs change may be needed:

- Participants not showing up
- Conversation not staying on topic
- Participant or guide feels disrespected or not listened to, especially more than once
- A pattern of not living into the covenant arises
- Evaluation tools indicate no growth or change in attitudes or behaviors

APPENDIX H

Evaluations

The following evaluation tools are templates that youth leaders can adapt and use for their Covenant Discipleship groups. Evaluation should be done regularly so that a picture of growth over time can become clear.

"Who Do You Say That I Am?"

Each participant rates on a scale of 1–5 how much they agree with each statement. The statements provided are explicitly about God, Jesus, and the Holy Spirit—however, this tool could easily be modified to include a church's mission, vision, or values statements.

On a scale of 1–5, rate how much you agree or disagree with each statement:
1 = Not at All, 5 = Totally

1. When I choose to act like Jesus, God transforms me.

   1   2   3   4   5

2. When I choose to act like Jesus, God works through me to transform the world.

    1   2   3   4   5

3. I am familiar with Jesus' life and teachings.

    1   2   3   4   5

4. I am confident that I can live out Jesus' teachings.

    1   2   3   4   5

5. I have had more chances to act like Jesus because of my Covenant Discipleship group.

    1   2   3   4   5

6. I understand what it means to live a life of discipleship.

    1   2   3   4   5

7. I can easily identify places and people that need compassion and or justice in my community.

    1   2   3   4   5

8. I do and experience acts of devotion regularly.

    1   2   3   4   5

9. I do and experience acts of worship regularly.

    1   2   3   4   5

10. I see the work of God in the world around me.

    1   2   3   4   5

11. I have sensed the guidance of the Holy Spirit.

    1   2   3   4   5

"How Is It with Your Soul?"

Each participant in a group fills in the first column with the clauses from their covenant.

Covenant Clause	How important is this to my personal faith development? 1 = not at all 3 = could live without 5 = must have	How important is this for my community? 1 = not at all 3 = could live without 5 = must have	How often do I do this thing? 1 = almost never 2 = 3-4 times a year 3 = once or twice a month 4 = weekly 5 = daily
Compassion 1:			
Compassion 2:			
Justice 1:			
Justice 2:			
Devotion 1:			
Devotion 2:			
Worship 1:			
Worship 2:			
Misc:			
Misc:			

What are the most impactful experiences you've had related to the clauses in your group's covenant?

Where Are You? (Relational Surface Area and Cultural Exegesis)

Participants write their own answers and stories on this evaluation tool.

1. How many chances have I had in the past week to do something intentional for my own faith?

2. How many chances have I had in the past week to be in conversation with someone else from my youth ministry or church?

3. How many chances have I had in the past week to act like or share Jesus in my community?

4. What have I discovered about compassion and relationships with God and other people during my time as a covenant disciple?

5. What have I discovered about justice and relationships with God and other people during my time as a covenant disciple?

6. What have I discovered about devotion and relationships with God and other people during my time as a covenant disciple?

7. What have I discovered about worship and relationships with God and other people during my time as a covenant disciple?

8. Where have I seen God, Jesus, or the Holy Spirit at work in myself in the past week?

9. Where have I seen God, Jesus, or the Holy Spirit at work in my church in the past week?

10. Where have I seen God, Jesus, or the Holy Spirit at work in my community in the past week?

11. Where have I seen God, Jesus, or the Holy Spirit at work in the world in the past week?

12. In my group of friends, a current cultural issue is _____. What would God want me to say or do with that issue?

COVENANT DISCIPLESHIP GLOSSARY

the General Rule of Discipleship. "To witness to Jesus Christ in the world, and to follow his teachings through acts of compassion, justice, worship, and devotion under the guidance of the Holy Spirit." This General Rule is the foundation of Covenant Discipleship groups. It is derived from the General Rules. Both are found in *The Book of Discipline of The United Methodist Church*.

balanced discipleship. The General Rule of Discipleship helps Covenant Discipleship groups maintain balance between all the teachings of Jesus and mitigates against focusing only on those teachings persons are temperamentally inclined toward. The General Rule helps persons practice both works of piety (acts of worship and acts of devotion) *and* works of mercy (acts of compassion and acts of justice). It also guides persons to attend to the personal dimensions of discipleship (acts of compassion and acts of devotion) *and* the public (acts of justice and acts of worship). The General Rule of Discipleship is inclusive and practicable.

witness. A witness testifies to the truth. A witness has personal experience with a person or event. The experience of witnesses enables them to tell others about the one they know. Christians are baptized, called, and equipped to witness to Jesus Christ in the world. We witness to what Jesus witnessed to: the reign of God that is breaking out in the world and that is coming.

Jesus' teachings. Jesus summarized his teachings in Matthew 22:37-40: " 'You shall love the Lord your God with all your heart, and with all your soul, and with all your mind.' This is the greatest and first commandment. And a second is like it: 'You shall love your neighbor as yourself.' On these two commandments hang all the law and the prophets." The General Rule of Discipleship and the covenant groups write are intended to help Christians obey Jesus' teachings.

acts of compassion. The simple acts of kindness we do for another person. For example, when we meet someone who is hungry, the act of compassion is to give him or her something to eat.

acts of justice. The actions Christians participate in with others, as communities of faith, to address the systemic and institutional causes of our neighbor's suffering. Christ calls us not only to help a person who is suffering but also to ask why the person is suffering and then to act to address the causes of injustice.

acts of worship. What Christians do together to offer themselves in service to God through praise, prayer, hymn, confession, forgiveness, scripture, proclamation, and sacrament.

acts of devotion. The practices Christians do alone to nurture and participate in their personal relationship with God: daily prayer and Bible reading, centering prayer, keeping a journal, intercessory prayer, devotional reading, writing, and fasting or abstinence.

covenant. Each Covenant Discipleship group writes a covenant shaped by the General Rule of Discipleship. The covenant serves as the agenda for the weekly meeting. It has three essential parts: preamble, a list of up to ten clauses, and a conclusion. The preamble is a shared statement of the shared faith in Christ and the purpose of the covenant. The clauses are balanced between acts of compassion, justice, worship, and devotion and appear in the same order in which the practices are named in the General Rule of Discipleship. The conclusion is a brief statement reaffirming the nature of the covenant and group members' shared dependence upon grace to live the Christian life.

accountability. Covenant Discipleship groups are accountability groups. They meet weekly for one hour for mutual accountability and support for discipleship guided by the covenant they have written and shaped by the General Rule of Discipleship. Accountability practiced in these groups is simply each member giving an account of what he or she has done, or not done, in light of the group's covenant. It is telling stories about how the group member has lived the Christian life since the last meeting, guided by the group's covenant. The leader, and other group members, can ask questions. The purpose of accountability is to "watch over one another in love" and to help one another grow and mature in holiness of heart and life; loving God with all our heart, soul, and mind, and loving those whom God loves, as God loves them.

weekly meetings. Covenant Discipleship groups meet weekly for one hour. Experience tells us that the weekly meeting is essential. It is the best way for the group to help one another grow in discipleship through accountability and support. Children's Covenant Discipleship groups meet for one and a half to two hours each week to accommodate acts of compassion and justice.

REFERENCES

"Baptismal Covenant I," *The United Methodist Hymnal*, The United Methodist Publishing House, 1989.

The Book of Discipline of The United Methodist Church 2008. Nashville: Abingdon, 2009.

Covenant Prayer, *The Complete Works of the Reverend John Wesley, A.M.*, 3rd ed., Vol. 2. London: John Mason, 1829.

"A Covenant with God." The Methodist Church in Britain. http://www.methodist.org.uk/who-we-are/what-is-distinctive-about-methodism/a-covenant-with-god.

Fink, Roger, and Rodney Stark. *The Churching of America, 1776–2005: Winners and Losers in Our Religious Economy*. New Brunswick, NJ: Rutgers UP, 2005.

"Social Principles." General Board of Church and Society of The United Methodist Church, The United Methodist Publishing House, 2012; http://umc-gbcs.org/social-principles.

Iovino, Joe. "How's Your Spiritual Life? The Class Meeting for Today," What We Believe. United Methodist Church, August 17, 2015. http://www.umc.org/what-we-believe/hows-your-spiritual-life-the-class-meeting-for-today.

Land Use table, "Resources," *FAO Statistical Yearbook*. Food and Agriculture Organization of the United Nations, 2010. http://www.fao.org/economic/ess/ess-publications/ess-yearbook/ess-yearbook2010/yearbook2010-reources/en/.

Manskar, Steven W. *Accountable Discipleship: Living in God's Household*. Discipleship Resources, 2003.

"Our Social Creed." *The Book of Discipline of The United Methodist Church 2012.* Nashville: United Methodist Publishing House, 2012. http://www.umc.org/what-we-believe/our-social-creed.

The Services of the Baptismal Covenant in The United Methodist Church: As Revised to Align with the 2008 Book of Discipline and Book of Resolutions. Nashville: General Board of Discipleship of The United Methodist Church, 2009.

Watson, Kevin. *The Class Meeting: Reclaiming a Forgotten (and Essential) Small Group Experience.* Seedbed Publishing, 2013.

Werner, David. "John Wesley's Question: "How Is Your Doing?" *The Asbury Journal* 65, no. 2, 68–93.

Wesley, John. "Advice to a People Called Methodist," *The Works of John Wesley,* Thomas Jackson edition, 1872. http://www.umcmission.org/Find-Resources/John-Wesley-Sermons/The-Wesleys-and-Their-Times/Advice-to-a-People-Called-Methodist.

———. "The Character of a Methodist," *The Works of John Wesley,* Thomas Jackson edition, 1872. http://www.umcmission.org/Find-Resources/John-Wesley-Sermons/The-Wesleys-and-Their-Times/The-Character-of-a-Methodist#sthash.AYWQUOIx.dpuf.

———. *A Plain Account of the People Called Methodist* (p. 259). Vol. 9 of *The Works of John Wesley.* Thomas Jackson edition. London: Wesleyan Methodist Book Room, 1872; Franklin, TN: Providence House, 1995.

———. *Primitive Physic, or an Easy and Natural Method of Curing Most Diseases.* London: 1774.

———. Sermon 98, "On Visiting the Sick."

———. *Thoughts upon Methodism* (p. 528). Vol. 9 of *The Works of John Wesley.* Thomas Jackson edition. London: Wesleyan Methodist Book Room, 1872; Franklin, TN: Providence House , 1995.

"Why It's Hard to Change Unhealthy Behavior—and Why You Should Keep Trying." Harvard Women's Health Watch, January 2007. http://www.health.harvard.edu/staying-healthy/why-its-hard-to-change-unhealthy-behavior.

Wigger, John. *American Saint Francis Asbury and the Methodists.* Oxford University Press, 2009.